Self-Harm/Injury
An Exploration Of Attitudes And Issues From Literature And Personal Stories

I0104279

Bruce Wallace

chipmunkapublishing
the mental health publisher

Published by
Chipmunkapublishing
PO Box 6872
Brentwood
Essex CM13 1ZT
United Kingdom

http://www.chipmunkapublishing.com

Copyright © Bruce Wallace 2012
Edited by Joelyn Rolston-Esdelle
ISBN   978-1-84991-765-0

Chipmunkapublishing gratefully acknowledge the support of Arts Council England.

Contents:

Diagrams:

Acknowledgements

For the groups and individuals who advised, supported and responded so positively – thank you.

For those individuals who contributed – a major thank you for your trust and willingness to provide some of your most personal experiences to a complete stranger. I hope that I have repaid your commitment (at least in part) through the completion of this work.

Glossary of Abbreviations

A&E:	Accident and Emergency Department
BPD:	Borderline Personality Disorder
CAMHS:	Child and Adolescent Mental Health Services
CBT:	Cognitive Behavioural Therapy
CPN:	Community Psychiatric Nurse
DSM:	Diagnostic and Statistical Manual of Mental Disorders
GP:	General Practitioner
ICD:	International Statistical Classification of Diseases and Related Health Problems
NHS:	National Health Service
NICE:	National Institute for Clinical Excellence
PE:	Physical Education
PSHE:	Personal, Social and Health Education
PTSD:	Post-Traumatic Stress Disorder
RAMH:	Renfrewshire Association for Mental Health
SI:	Self-injury

Self-Harm/Injury

Background

The journey undertaken to complete this book began a very long time ago. As a mental health nurse who qualified in the early 1970's my practice was heavily influenced by the thinking of the day. In the areas of acute mental health units and acute admission wards that I had originally worked in, it was not unusual to encounter people admitted who had been involved in activities that resulted in self-harm/injury. Much of the discussion then revolved around issues of suicide and attempted suicide as the primary intention. Any activities that resulted in what was perceived by practitioners as limited physical harm/injury (e.g. superficial cutting; overdose of medication and subsequent presentation for help/support) was widely regarded as 'attention seeking behaviour' and not as a 'real' attempt to die. This was unfortunately not an unusual response by practitioners within a number of caring professions who had little awareness, insight or experience at that time regarding self-harm/injury.

It was only later with the emergence of a growing body of literature on the subject together with a realisation that not everyone who self-harmed/injured had an automatic association with suicide, that practitioners started to question their knowledge and competence in what was perceived by many to be a new area of practice. I had an awareness of self-harm/injury as an issue but this was not developed to any significant extent in practice. It was not until I began teaching and became responsible for facilitating a module within my university that I started to explore the subject in much more detail. As my contacts with staff, colleagues, and students undertaking the module and initial communication with support groups developed, it was obvious that my own knowledge and understanding of the subject needed to be developed.

This resulted in an invitation to a number of support groups to provide input into the programme and provide the mainly professional staff (and myself) with an awareness of the needs, aspirations and concerns of individuals who self-harmed/injured. Although a range of groups were contacted, two in particular became a regular and invaluable resource in supporting the programme and helping numerous students develop a greater understanding of what is frequently referred to as the user or expert perspective. This is now seen as very important particularly in health and social care where it is now recognised that the 'expert' is not the professional but rather the person experiencing the situation, illness or condition.

These two particular organisations became regular contributors and helped both students and myself to develop a greater appreciation of many of the issues faced by the individuals with whom they were in contact. FirstSigns and the Samaritans are the two groups who I owe a debt of gratitude to for helping to influence the students' perceptions of self-harm/injury. In addition to this, they provided me with a greater awareness and insight into some of the important issues related to the area.

Over a number of years it also became more obvious that something of a dichotomy existed in the type of information generally available. In the professional arena this was most marked by the development of a steady increase in the number and diversity of research articles and material that was beginning to emerge. By contrast support groups and other organisations were creating a wealth of material based on an individual's own experiences - what has become known as 'lived experience' - of self-harm/injury. At the time there was also some published material emerging that integrated both research and experiences based on the organisation or group's own work. Although some of the material contained reference to the experiences of some individuals, there appeared to be a lack of detailed accounts other than those provided by individuals on other more specific websites. These were frequently perceived to be a way of communicating with other users on that site and as a way of seeking, sharing and offering support.

The culmination of these observations was a recognition that there existed the opportunity of trying to combine some of the information that reflected a professional perspective, together with a platform that enabled individuals to provide their own specific and unique experiences through the medium of their stories. My own professional and educational background gave me one perspective but failed to provide me with the detailed insight and knowledge to attempt to explain self-harm/injury from the perspective of an individual who has experienced it.

After the decision was taken to write the book it became apparent that there was a need to try to identify and gather the necessary information that would attempt to reflect some of the various perspectives mentioned. In order to facilitate this, a range of individuals and organisations were contacted with a view to exploring whether the people who self-harmed/injured were willing to share their experiences with a view to helping others to develop a greater understanding and awareness through telling their story. To enable as broad an opportunity as possible within a relatively short time, it was determined that the use of emails was the most convenient method of communication with agencies and contacts already identified. This would allow rapid communication with some of the organisations both in this country and overseas. In addition, there was a degree of anonymity in this medium that allowed people sufficient distance when contacted, to decide without any expectation or pressure whether they wished to support the planned undertaking or not.

Emails were despatched over a twelve-month period, together with an outline of the plan, intention and invitation to contact me for further clarification and information as deemed appropriate. The initial response was rather disheartening as little interest appeared to be shown. Although on reflection this was probably my own impatience rather than the unwillingness of people to get involved.

A gentle reminder from one of the initial contacts to persevere helped me maintain the enthusiasm needed, and gradually responses started to appear. The use of email, newsletters and blogs by contacted groups (to name just a few of the methods employed) were now generating responses and individual enquiries. In addition, some organisations indicated that they did not have direct contact with individuals who self-harmed/injured and if they did it was on an anonymous basis meaning that they could not be contacted. In these situations many of the individuals contacted provided alternative ideas for me to explore that was very much appreciated.

Online groups such as TangledWeb, S.A.S.H, Self-harm (Luton) and inspireireland all deserve a mention for their advice and support during this period. Their links enabled me to contact a broad range of individuals and subsequent other contacts to maintain the momentum.

Options had been employed to enable individuals to respond. They could make contact with a specific group that they were already familiar with to enable responses to be collated and forwarded to me. Details were also forwarded by email for individual contact with regards to their interest and willingness to become involved through telling their story.

Introduction

Self-harming has become a much more prominent issue during the last couple of decades. It is not a new phenomenon and has been an issue for some considerable time but unfortunately has not been identified within the public arena. The gradual emergence of a 'problem' associated with a behaviour where people (more often than not identified as young) physically harm or injure themselves created an interest in a range of health, social, educational and voluntary agencies. This in turn led to the growth of a body of information and expressed interest in exploring the subject in terms of whom, what, and why.

A greater awareness on the topic of self-harming/injuring has led to an extensive range of research activity and the publication of material in a wide range of journals, books, reports and other media. Some of the literature that is now available indicates that the incidence of self-harm/injury has increased and that here in the United Kingdom we have some of the highest incidence rates in Europe. Estimates vary due to the fact that many people do not tell others that they are self-harming/injuring, or avoid contact with services due to some negative experiences that they have personally encountered or reported by people they know.

An inclination on the part of 'professional' literature - particularly health - to explore self-harm/injury either in the context of mental illness or suicide and suicide risk has not necessarily endeared this material to some people who may be seeking support. They may not consider themselves to have a mental illness or to be contemplating suicide. Although literature exploring self-harm/injury frequently identifies a correlation in mental illness/possible suicide risk and social groups (e.g. Goths) these are not the elements being explored in any significant detail within this book. They will be incorporated to some extent as it is inevitable that some individuals will be associated with both self-harm/injury and mental illness or suicide. Although it is an uncomfortable association, the fact that it exists and people research and publish a wealth of material identifying correlations means that to maintain a balanced perspective all contemporary views need to be acknowledged, even if they are not necessarily accepted or approved of by others.

How practitioners are trained and their awareness and responses to those who have self-harmed/injured is another area that has received an increasing degree of attention. Some material explore the experiences of people who have sought help and support from practitioners as a means of determining whether services are improving in their treatment of and attitude toward the concept of self-harming/injuring and the individuals who seek help and/or support after having self-harmed/injured.

An alternative stream of information has emerged from sources other than the 'professional' literature and acts somewhat as a counterbalance. This is now widespread and a significant amount of this information is now available. Some of it may be based on surveys carried out by groups from a voluntary or support organisation. Other sources include the individual publication of personal experiences by people who have self-harmed/injured. The information produced may be in the form of books, booklets, articles, reports, DVDs, online forums or indeed training provided by groups and/or individuals. This is now widely available through a growing range of organisations and groups who provide support by way of direct and/or internet contact, literature, and the provision of training to a diverse range of audiences.

The audiences mentioned tend to consist of people who are increasingly interested in extending both their knowledge of the area and potentially their skills for supporting individuals. These include those working or associated with professional groups, together with a range of voluntary, independent and private agencies. It is important to consider that also included are people such as family members, friends and colleagues of the individual who may be self-harming/injuring. They may be searching for an understanding and awareness outside of the boundaries that they currently live or work within as this might be too difficult, challenging or distressing for the individuals involved at a specific point in time.

What is not in doubt is that many people do self-harm/injure. They come from a wide range of backgrounds and experiences, age ranges, ethnicities and include both males and females. There is no one profile to offer by way of a simple explanation of who may self-harm/injure or why. The focus of this book will be to enable some of those very individuals who have self-harmed an opportunity of telling their own unique story in the hope that the reader will become more aware of the diversity of both individuals and experiences that are reflected in this often misunderstood area. It will also identify and explore some of the issues raised within the multitude of literature and other sources of information on the subject that now exist.

Many of the mainstream services such as education and health have attempted to improve the individual's experience through the training and education of staff working within those areas. A greater understanding is present and people are now more aware that the person who may make an appointment with their General Practitioner (GP) or talk to their teacher or lecturer about having self-harmed/injured are often extremely vulnerable. This vulnerability is now being more readily recognised and has led to a gradual improvement in the way professionals engage with the person. The need to be sensitive, non-judgemental and offer the person both privacy and the opportunity to talk about their needs is now much more widely recognised and practiced. Part of the ongoing difficulty facing staff attempting to understand and respond appropriately to individuals who do self-harm/injure is that these very individuals add to the complexity by indicating that the reasons they may be engaging in this behaviour are many and varied. Much of what we read tends to suggest that self-harm is about injuring yourself through cutting. This may be one of the ways – the most commonly reported - but there are a multitude of different ways people might harm/injure themselves. These could include such diverse activities as; hair pulling, burning skin, breaking bones or taking an overdose. Some individuals may engage in more than one form of harming/injuring themselves depending on the emotional 'trigger'; e.g. anger or distress.

It is also important to ensure that individuals who may self-harm/injure but do not necessarily have the opportunity of communicating their experiences to a wider audience when in need (e.g. in prison, acute mental health unit, learning disability service provision) are effectively supported by staff that have received appropriate training and possess the knowledge and skills to provide effective and meaningful assistance. This can, on occasion be enhanced through training provided by the very individuals who have/are self-harming/injuring. This is demonstrated quite nicely in an interesting article published recently by Moores (2011), a service user with a learning disability, who was supported to publish his story with the aid of members of staff in the facility where he lives.

References:
Moores P with Fish R and Duperouzel H (2011) 'I can try and do my little bit' – training staff about self-injury, *Journal of Learning Disabilities and Offending Behaviour*, Volume 2, Issue 1, pp4-7

WHY USE THE TERM SELF-HARM/INJURY IN THIS BOOK?

The decision to use the joint self-harm/injury title for this specific piece of work has resulted from an awareness that the expressions used to reflect this area are many and varied. There is an acknowledgement that many of the terms still visible within the published literature are not appreciated by individuals who harm/injure themselves and that some of the 'old' terminology that has been discarded in some areas still surfaces within some of the literature (e.g. deliberate self-harm).

It was recognised that some individuals regarded any external physical evidence (e.g. cutting) as an injury whereas an overdose of medication (no external physical evidence) was harm. The difficulty with this concept is the potential overlap where an individual may carry out an action (e.g. insertion of needles under the skin) that may not be appear immediately visible in one person (except through investigations such as x-ray) but visible in another leading to the question of what actually constitutes self-harm as opposed to self-injury? Is it purely based on visible external evidence or do we adopt a more flexible approach to it and if so are we not only adding to the confusion that already exists in many peoples' minds regarding this.

There was some discussion based around the fact that combining the terms was rather 'long winded' and yet another expression to add to the already lengthy list. Due consideration was given to this and many other comments that were offered and although challenging were accepted and appreciated. The need to allow individuals to comment and input was again regarded as an essential part of the process of attempting to ensure that views and opinions were both listened to and incorporated in the process.

In addition to discussions with a range of colleagues and other individuals a range of literature was accessed and explored in an attempt to clarify potential terminology. Rather than reduce the potential for confusion this resulted in an extended range of both terminology (refer to list on page 15) and variations in definitions of the same or similar terminology. Much of the literature uses self-harm as the primary term but variations occur.

Examples include Pembroke (1996) who indicated that: "The term 'Deliberate Self-Harm' is objectionable. …How self-harm occurs and the levels of awareness vary considerably. Self-harm or self-injury does not require qualifying with '**Deliberate**'"(p6). Hawton et al in their Oxford Report on Deliberate Self-Harm (2008) meanwhile utilise the term deliberate self-harm but in its specific identification and exploration of method used separated this term into self-poisoning and self-injury (p14).

Duffy (2006) indicated that self-injury was a distinct behaviour in its own right and therefore not the same as self-harm. By way of contrast Horrocks et al (2003) explore the concept of self-harm, separating it into a number of categories; the principle two being self-injury and self-poisoning - this despite the title of the article being self-injury.

The organisation FirstSigns separates out the two elements and qualifies their distinction quite effectively as follows:
'Self-harm is an umbrella term that includes a variety of behaviours that damage, or cause harm to a person. Self-injury falls under the umbrella of self-harm, and is a direct behaviour that causes injury and damage to one's body. At FirstSigns, we believe the intention of self-injury is to release tension and seek relief from distress; we focus on the intention and the fact that people rely on self-injury as a coping mechanism.'

Alderman (2009) in a piece entitled 'Self-Injury: Does it Matter What It's Called?' explores the wide variations in terminology and suggests that a unified term is appropriate and supports that of self-injury. MIND in their booklet also acknowledge the fact that self-harm is a broad term but then explain it thus: 'Self-harm is a broad term. People may injure or poison themselves by scratching, cutting or burning their skin, by hitting themselves against objects, taking a drug overdose, or swallowing or putting other things inside themselves.'

Myer (2011) in her article introduces a number of different terms including intentional self-injury and self-injurious behaviour (SIB) and defines SIB as: 'self-harming behaviors used to cope with intense, uncomfortable emotions.' (p26)

Chandler et al (2011) extracts the term 'self-injury' from the large range of terminology used in a rather confusing overlap of interpretations. They ascribe the following meaning: 'intentional injury to the outside of the body, mainly through cutting, but including scratching burning, biting, or hitting.' (p99) They retain a focus on self-injury and challenge the difficulty encountered when attempting to clearly extricate self-harm from a number of activities that are not perceived to have a 'clinical' component or outcome (e.g. reckless behaviour).

By way of raising awareness of the many expressions that can still be widely identified, a scan of relatively recent literature published on the subject in different countries identified a range of expressions. These appear in the following list:

- Deliberate self-harm
- Deliberate non-suicidal self-harm
- Deliberate self-injury syndrome
- Self-mutilation
- Self-Injurious behaviour

- Intentional self-injury
- Intentional self-harm
- Parasuicide
- Cutting
- Self-abuse
- Non-suicidal self-injury
- Non-suicidal self-harm
- Non-fatal suicidal behaviour
- Self-injury
- Self-harm

I am aware that I am in effect adding to this elongated list but have been guided by the recognition that the individuals who I have liaised with appear to have very strongly held views regarding the activity they have engaged in and what they consider it reflects and should be referred to. Others may hold equally strong and valid views regarding this but I recognise that terminology will undoubtedly continue evolving with more changes to come. What is evident is that it is all too easy to become distracted by the terminology in an attempt to identify more specifically what the key elements are. In doing that, it is possible to become fixated with labelling and potentially overlooking the person as the primary focus, not the label.

Ultimately the decision to combine the two terms was identified and accepted in recognition of the division of thinking that appears to exist. However it may be pertinent to finish this section by acknowledging that despite the uncertainty that prevails in what is the 'right' and 'wrong' terminology, it is important to recognise that for the person who is involved in the process 'it is what they say it is'.

References:

Alderman T (2009) *Self-Injury: Does it Matter What It's Called?*, The Scarred Soul Blogs, WebMD

Duffy DF (2006) Self-injury, *Psychiatry*, Volume 5, Issue 8, pp263-265

Hawton K, Casey D, Bale E, Shepherd A, Bergen H, Simkin S, *Deliberate Self-Harm in Oxford* (2008) Oxford, Centre for Suicide Research

Horrocks J, Price S, House A & Owens D (2003) Self-injury attendances in the accident and emergency department: Clinical database study, *The British Journal of Psychiatry*, 183, pp34-39

Myer T (2011) Inside Intentional Self-injury, *Nursing*, 26-31

Pembroke LR (Ed)(1996) *Self-Harm: Perspectives from Personal Experience*, Survivors Speak Out

STORIES

The stories volunteered by individuals will be spread throughout the book to ensure that they maintain the profile that they deserve. It is important for the reader to acknowledge that the surrounding material is of value but should not detract attention from the reality of self-harm/injury. It will also ensure that the reader recognises how unique self-harm/injury is to each and every individual who experiences it.

There is no particular priority in terms of where stories have been introduced within the book. They provide the reader with a candid account of how each individual has encountered and dealt with a range of different experiences. I have not altered any of the content save for some details linked to individual's names and geographical location to maintain confidentiality as this was indicated in the original correspondence.

I hope that when you read each story you can appreciate the courage that was needed for each person to provide such a personal account of their life and experiences to ensure that others could hopefully understand the subject of self-harm/injury a little more clearly and appreciate how it affects each and every person involved.

The importance of the above information is the fact that individuals and groups have been prepared to communicate across a diverse range of agencies with one common agenda which has resulted in this book's most important element; i.e. the 'stories'.

Ma [age 29]

2009, 2 strange things happened; 1st, I turned 28 and 2nd, I found out that I'm going to be a dad again! Probably doesn't sound too strange but believe you me, it is.

17 years old I was living on the streets of south London, drug problem, drink problem, not caring about anything or anyone, doing what I had to do in order to stay alive. That's quite strange as well actually. 5 years before that I had everything; a loving family, a home, plans for the future and ok, I was still a bit of a lad but I wasn't so bad.

"You killed her, the stress you caused was what killed her" That's what I was told, no love or support, just those words which have haunted me ever since. You see, in 1998 my Mum lost her long battle with cancer, leaving behind myself, my brother and our Dad. It's not nice watching your Mum slowly die from cancer, the sickness from chemotherapy, the tiredness from the radiotherapy. Waking up in the morning, going down for breakfast and seeing your Mum crying and pulling out clumps of hair, visiting her in a hospice and having her not even know who you are, swollen beyond recognition due to medication. All this and she was only 38. First it was breast cancer which she managed to beat, only to find out a year later that it was in her brain, any treatment would be a waste of time; just go away and die.

I had been self harming since I was about 11, just little scratches here and there, but still, self-harming all the same. I never told anyone and no one ever asked. The joy of having a special needs brother meant that I was just left to get on with things, no one ever really paid much attention to what I was doing. After my

Mum died I went to see my GP as I was really struggling, I couldn't sleep, eat, do anything. I had started to cut myself rather than just giving myself little scratches. His answer, pills, nothing else, just pills. So I started to take these little pills and then discovered that if I drank alcohol whilst taking them I had one of the best highs ever! It was great, well, that's how it felt at the time. After a while the high went away and I found myself in search of something else to give me back that high. You know what; no matter what I took I always found it to be 100 times better mixed with alcohol! And so the addictions began.

Shortly after, I was thrown out of the 'family' home by my Dad for reasons that I'm still unsure of to this day, but hey, that's a different story. For a while I kipped on friend's sofas and floors, shop doors, underpasses, building sites, you get the picture. All the time using whatever drug I could get my hands on and making sure I didn't sober up. This went on for a couple of years, 2 years of drink and drug abuse. Somehow, I managed to secure a job in a pub, yep a pub!! Result!!!!!!!!!! The good thing was, it came with a small flat as well. Things started to go well for a while, well when I say well, I was warm and had a kitchen! Even stranger than securing a job I found myself in a relationship which was really weird, a drunken addict in a relationship. It was doomed from the beginning.

Well it was during that relationship that I realised that there was something REALLY wrong in my head. At this point I was cutting several times a day, every day. I had managed to knock the drugs on the head but I was still very much an alcoholic. For some reason my partner at the time must have seen something worth fighting for because we ended up moving in together. Despite me trying to change and make things work I couldn't, there was something wrong with me, something really wrong. This relationship lasted just shy of 2 years and ended very badly. Towards the end I was being admitted to hospital on a weekly basis, overdose after overdose and serious self-harming. Despite all the hospital admissions, I was never assessed by a CPN or anyone in the mental health sector.

When the relationship ended I completely lost it and ended up taking a mixture of 50+ pills. I don't really remember a lot about that day, just waking up in hospital with tubes and wires coming out of me and going into me, I don't think there was a vein or orifice which didn't have a tube or needle in it! I was told afterwards that CPR was needed and I was very lucky to still be alive. Very lucky eh? Yeah right! So lucky that they sectioned me! Not what I needed, not what I needed at all. You may think that I spent weeks in the hospital, you'll be wrong. Through my 'travels' I had learnt quite a bit, I knew exactly what I had to say to the doctors, I knew exactly what they wanted to hear, I knew the words to use and how to use them. So, I talked the talk and get released from hospital, back to an empty flat I went, stopping off at my dealers on the way. That was the start of my next period of addiction and homelessness.

After a few weeks, my little brother came to my rescue! My little brother came to my rescue; shouldn't that be the other way round?! Anyway I made the move from London to Gloucestershire. With the help of my brother I was able to find a job and a flat. For a while things were going well, I was managing to hold down a job, I was still using, drinking and cutting but I was managing to hide it. If only it could have lasted.

The summer came and people were curious as to why I always wore long sleeved tops I tried my best to avoid the questions, it was so hard, what was I to tell them? Even my brother didn't know what I was doing to myself, that's how good I was at hiding it. 6 weeks after moving with my brother, getting the job and the flat I blew it all AGAIN! People found out that I was self harming, my drinking and drug use spiralled out of control and I was evicted from my flat. It's strange how one thing affects another; I was evicted from my flat and then lost my job, all within a few hours. I was 'laid' off as I had no fixed abode!!

So again I was homeless only this time it was completely different! I was used to being on the streets in London, the 1st change I was aware of was how bloody cold it was! The only way to combat that... yep, even more drink and drugs. Doing whatever I had to in order to survive and taking whatever I could get my hands on. During my time in Gloucestershire I never saw anyone regarding my mental health, I wasn't receiving any form of treatment - except from my self-medicating!

Skipping forward a few years to 2004 my life changed. To be exact, it was the 25th February 2004. That was when I became a father for the first time. Everything changed I was determined to become a different person, a better person. No drink, no drugs and no self-harming. Just like that I stopped it all, I was cured, I done it!

I lasted a couple of hours...

Who was I kidding; I couldn't stop just like that, no chance. I plucked up the courage to go and speak to my GP. That was one of the best decisions I've ever made. I told him everything, the drinking, drugs and self-harm. Straight away he prescribed a heavy course of anti depressants and made a referral to hospital for an assessment. I left his surgery with strict instructions to go and see him the moment I feel like doing something stupid, even if I just needed someone to scream at, go and see him.

I went home and started taking the pills, after all, I had been there before hadn't I," just take the pills". There was something different this time though; I was taking them as they were prescribed. I was still drinking but not the amounts I had been. Something inside me had changed, I suppose it was that this time I did actually want to get better and get help. By some miracle I was managing to stay off the drugs, not sure how but I was. A week or so after going to my GP I received my appointment for the hospital. It was at that point that my anxiety levels went through the roof!

Having to go back to the 'nuthouse' what if they sectioned me again, what if they took my boy off of me; everyone knows that the system doesn't work.

Despite this, I went to the appointment and guess what; they let me go home again!!! I was really surprised with how it had gone. It was acknowledged that I had some serious issues that needed addressing and that I wouldn't get better over night. The shrink at the hospital referred me for something called cognitive behavioural therapy (CBT) a load of crap, I thought at the time. They were going to change the way I thought? Yeah right!

So, CBT and antidepressants, the combination was starting to show signs of working, I was given techniques to use instead of self-harming, still no drug use and managing to control the drinking. Things were going well, so I thought anyway. 1 step forward 3 steps backwards that was me! Just as I thought I was making progress I started to have nightmares. It was always the same one. My mum's face, it would start normal and then change; it would change dramatically resulting in me seeing maggots coming out of it before it burst into flames! Freaky, I know!! If the dreams weren't bad enough it started happening when I was awake, I would see my mum's face when out shopping etc and it would transform as it did in the nightmare.

That must have tipped me over the edge, back came the drink and the self-harming, on a positive note however, I was still off the drugs. That was me, back at the hospital for another assessment! It turned out that the assessment would change everything for me again;

I was finally given a diagnosis. Don't know if you had noticed but until then I was never diagnosed with anything!

Depressive Psychotic Episodes
Adverse Grief Reaction
Depressive Personality
Depression
Anxiety
Post Traumatic Stress Disorder

I'll touch briefly on the PTSD as that's the main reason for my anxiety. I mentioned that I done whatever it took to survive on the streets, well, I saw some things, horrible things...

So I had all these things wrong with me, I was screwed! Back to CBT I went with all these problems. Strangely, my therapist said that it wasn't as bad as it sounded, most of them could all be wrapped up into one and dealt with at the same time. She said that the hardest one to deal with would be the anxiety. So I carried on with the meds and the CBT and after a while my dreams and hallucinations went away. The way I had to deal with them was strange. I was not allowed to brush the images to one side and forget about them, I had to 'analyse' them. Pick them apart and work out why I was seeing them. It worked, it was   decided that the change I was seeing in my mum's face was representative of the changes that actually happened to her, weird eh? Therefore making the nightmares, not scary! After a while they just disappeared.

I carried on with the CBT and found it to be really beneficial, anyways, I'm not doing this to promote CBT am I!

While I continued with the CBT and medication I continued on the 1 step forward and 2 steps backwards approach to things. My life and that of my long suffering partner were an ultimate rollercoaster ride. With ecstatic highs and the crippling lows that followed we never knew what to expect from one day to another. Even for me it was annoying and sometimes scary, the fact that when I was on a high I was very high, hyper even but then when the low came, and it always did, I struggled to get out of bed in the morning, struggled to look after myself, self harmed, had to fight the constant, and they were constant, thoughts of suicide. Even though the highs were better neither myself nor my partner were never able to enjoy them. We knew that it wouldn't last and soon I would come crashing back to earth with catastrophic results.

I must have done something right though as another baby came along. By the time that number 2 came along I had finished the CBT and was having no input from psych services. I was still on the antidepressants but that was it. Things were slightly better, I wasn't self-harming any more, I had combated the nightmares and hallucinations but I was far from being 'cured'. Things were completely different with my youngest son, I had thought things would be the same as they were 1st time round. I was unable to bond with him, I had no feelings for him whatsoever. I didn't know what was wrong with me, why could I be a dad to one child but not another? With those questions came panic attacks and heightened anxiety levels. It got to the point where I couldn't get on a bus or a train. Going shopping was damn near impossible, I couldn't go anywhere where I knew there would be crowds.

So, back to the doctors I went, tail between my legs, asking for more help. I say it like that because that was how it felt at the time. I had already asked for help and received the CBT, surely that should have been enough. My GP understood completely why I thought that and assured me that it was ok to ask for help whenever I needed it, "there are no magic wands, it takes time". Back to Dykebar I went for another assessment, this time I came away with a CPN. Not only did I get a CPN, I also had my antidepressants taken away from me. It was arranged that I would collect them 3 times a week from my chemist as I was not to have large quantities of pills at home, maybe the shrink and doc saw something I didn't? Anyway, I went home feeling like a naughty schoolboy!!

A week or so went by until my 1st CPN visit. I hadn't managed to make any progress with the baby, still no feelings etc. The 1st appointment with the CPN went quite well, we acknowledged that there were some more issues that we had to deal with, the main one being my anxiety and panic attacks. The whole not bonding thing could wait, neither I nor baby were going anywhere! Makes sense I suppose! So started the difficult job of combating my anxiety and panic attacks. I think it took around 18 months to make noticeable progress. A very long and very difficult journey, you know that saying "confront your fears"? Well, try doing that when you are scared of people!

Back when I was homeless, drunk and addicted I always thought that I would be dead before my 25th birthday and that I would never amount to anything, that's why, at the beginning of this story I referred to two strange things happening to me in 2009! To be 28, alive and not in prison is a massive achievement for me, not only that, I have 2 and a bit beautiful kids and an amazing partner, all of this and look where I came from! Some people call it 'recovery' some say 'being well'. I don't know what to call it so I'm going to go with, 'normal'. For the past 12 months I have been 'normal' and I'm loving it, I am able to do things I never thought possible! Ok, I'm not working, maybe I never will, I don't know, but I'm happy and able to enjoy life and my family. People like RAMH, my GP, CPN and my partner would probably like me to thank them for making me 'normal'

I'm not going to!

Yes, they may have supported me, they may have given me the skills needed to become 'normal' but, I done the work, not them and I combated my problems/fears on my own. I will be eternally grateful for the help and support they've given but I put in the hard work. In the past few weeks I have been discharged from the CPN's and psychiatry. The problems I had bonding with my youngest son, all sorted. I have learned not to plan ahead; I never plan more than a few days in advance. It saves disappointment. The only things I want for the future are to continue being 'normal', be the best dad and partner I can be and maybe even, try and give something back to people like RAMH.

At times it seemed impossible, at times I did give up, but hey, I guess I'm stronger than I thought I was.

WHAT IS SELF-HARM/INJURY?

It is reasonable to begin this work with an exploration of the subject area. The most logical starting point is the consideration of what self-harm/injury actually is or may be. This may appear relatively clear at an introductory level until you start reading the plethora of literature and exploring the other sources of information that have emerged and talk to a variety of people, (e.g. those who self-harm/injure, family, friends, colleagues, teachers, care professionals). Some of these will have direct experience of someone who has self-harmed/injured or alternatively are aware of the subject but have not had any direct experience with anyone who has self-harmed/injured.

What quickly emerges is that instead of a clearly identifiable construct a range of different views, opinions and indeed considerations arise which had not initially been incorporated into our thinking. These include, for example:

- Can self-harm be considered a 'normal' construct?
- If it can, under what circumstances?
- What differentiates that which is perceived as 'normal' from that deemed 'abnormal' in this context?
- Are the considerations involved always constant? i.e. is 'normal' or 'abnormal' always deemed 'normal' or 'abnormal'
- Is it something that deserves/requires/warrants 'acceptance' and if so, by whom, when and how?

Given these considerations it is not too difficult to understand the challenges that exist in attempting to clarify something that has so many variables. One of these is the difference apparent in how people in a diverse range of situations perceive self-harm/injury.

These include various groups and individuals including for example; practitioners (e.g. health & social care), professionals (e.g. teachers), the 'public', people who have direct personal experience of someone who has self-harmed/injured, and the media.

Everyone has an opinion or view and these can vary substantially. Some of them are based on experience while others are based on what has been said or written by others and either accepted or rejected. Part of the difficulty that has arisen is the dramatic increase in both publicity regarding the subject of self-harm/injury and emergence of a large body of information on the topic, not all of it 'singing from the same hymn sheet!' It is apparent from much of the literature explored in the preparation of this book that authors from similar practitioner and professional groups explore and identify a variety of different perspectives, not all of which demonstrate any degree of consistency.

One of the areas that often leads to confusion is that of what actually constitutes self-harm/injury. The author has had many conversations with colleagues in a range of health and social care roles and with individuals who have self-harmed/injured related to this very issue and a range of responses have emerged. One example of the difficulty that some people have in this context is that of separating out 'normal' behaviours and activities that cause harm or injury to that of the 'clinical' concept of self-harm/injury. The perception of self-harm/injury is recognised as something that changes based on variables such as society, culture, group, family and individual circumstances affecting how the person lives or what they subscribe to.

Even though there is a wide diversity of opinion on what self-harm/injury is, might be, or is not, does not mean it should not be explored. It is important to examine the concept from a range of different perspectives in an attempt to determine if there is common ground that can be identified. It is also something that may consist of a number of facets, not all regarded as 'problematic', at least not initially.

It is generally recognised and occasionally commented on that self-harm/injury is seen as a coping strategy, albeit a maladaptive or dysfunctional one. Watts (2011) in an online article exploring self-harm uses the term 'unhealthy', possibly less stigmatising than those offered above. This introduces the similarity that can be found in activities such as smoking and the consumption of alcohol. These can also on occasion be seen to play a role in terms of acting as coping strategies in a variety of different situations.

The distinction rests on the fact that the latter are still accepted as 'normal' within this society although, attitudes have started to change within the last decade in particular. Some of the issues acting as drivers within these changes are secondary rather than primary. They focus currently on the impact on others rather than self. For example there is a growing view that passive harm is unacceptable (linked to smoking) and that antisocial and risk escalating behaviour in a public domain (e.g. through alcohol consumption) that may place the individual and/or others at risk should be addressed. Sansome et al (2009) in their published study exploring self-harm behaviours add to the lack of clear boundaries by the utilisation of a 21-point self-harm inventory that includes, amongst others:

- Overdosed
- Cut yourself
- Burned yourself
- Abused alcohol
- Been promiscuous

It is also of interest to note that in the current draft guidelines that have been issued by NCCMH (April 2011) that the following distinction is made:

'the term self-harm is used in this guideline to refer to any act of self-poisoning or self-injury carried out by an individual irrespective of motivation (Hawton et al 2003a)... There are a number of important exclusions which this term is not intended to cover. These include harm to the self arising from excessive consumption of alcohol...'(p14).

It was frequently commented on that most people generally recognised that smoking cigarettes and consuming more than a 'reasonable' amount of alcohol are activities that could be clearly identified as self-harming. There are others - as mentioned later - but these two are regularly identified as leading to some confusion with that of the 'clinical' form of self-harm/injury because of the clear link with harm and on occasion injury. The distinction that is frequently used to separate some behaviour as 'acceptable' from those regarded as 'unacceptable' and therefore in need of potential intervention would appear to revolve around some of the following constructs (using smoking and alcohol consumption as examples):

1. Society still accepts and accommodates that smoking and drinking alcohol are acceptable although, attitudes have changed somewhat with the introduction of legislation that has restricted both in terms of when/where you can engage in the activity; for example smoke free and alcohol free zones prohibit the activity and anyone ignoring this may be prosecuted.
2. Self-harm is regarded as a side effect of the actual activity of smoking and/or drinking alcohol rather than part of the actual activity when it is taking place. The harm occurs at a later stage,

possibly many years later. This is usually associated with a clinical diagnosis (e.g. cancer, cirrhosis of the liver).

3. Intent – both of these activities are regarded as having a purpose that does not have its primary focus on self-harm/injury but on other motivational goals such as stress relief, social/group acceptance and/or belonging, or as a distraction technique. It is also recognised that there can be an addictive element associated with the activity.

It is interesting to note that point three bears a resemblance to some of the reasons provided by individuals for why they may self-harm/injure as identified later in the book, specifically issues related to stress relief and distraction. In addition there is work that suggests the abuse or acquired dependence on alcohol can exacerbate the risk of self-harming/injuring in individuals which further incorporates alcohol into the construct of self-harm/injury (e.g. Sinclair & Green, 2005)

Other behaviours that may be associated with the link to actual or potential self-harm/injury include such diverse activities as; body piercing, tattoos, placing oneself in a potentially dangerous situation (walking alone at night in a high risk area), or extended exposure to the summer sun in search of a tan without adequate skin protection. Again many people have involved themselves in at least one of the aforementioned activities but little attention appears to exist unless or until what is considered 'normal' is exceeded; e.g. extensive tattooing or body piercing. At this point people become what might be referred to as uncomfortable because of the extreme nature of the process as this can be readily observed. It is still not however considered as constituting something unacceptable in the same way that actual 'clinical' self-harm/injury is currently viewed.

It is obvious from this small range of examples offered that people frequently engage in what might be determined activities that have the potential for self-harm/injury but that they do not consider that this constitutes something unacceptable.

The use of the word 'clinical' identifies a specific association with professional categorization, specifically related to health or more accurately ill health. Much of the focus from a medical perspective that permeates much of the current approach in health care is related to the two international classifications used. It is useful to acknowledge these as they influence - to a large extent - the 'diagnostic' arena and place self-harm/injury within a clearly associated mental health context.

The diagnosis and classification of illness, particularly issues associated with mental illness are heavily reliant on the following two formats:

> DSM-IV (current version introduced 1994, revised 2000) [being reviewed and updated to DSM-V, planned for 2013]

This classification is linked to the American Psychiatric Association and used to identify a range of illnesses and/or conditions associated with 'mental disorder'. Currently within the DSM-IV classifications the only mention of 'self-mutilating' behaviour is in association with the section on Borderline Personality Disorder. The proposed change is the introduction of a section on what is termed non-suicidal self-injury (NSSI). This does not appear in the current version and demonstrates the recognition that self-harm/injury is not the same as suicide/attempted suicide and this has emerged within the rationale for this proposed change.

> ICD-10 (current version 2007, ICD-11 version planned for 2015)

This classification is linked to the World Health Organization and is associated with determining recognition or diagnosis in what is referred to as diseases and related health problems as indicated in the title. The chapter on intentional self-harm identifies a range of sub-sections including purposely self-inflicted poisoning, self-inflicted injury, suicide, attempted suicide. This is somewhat different to the proposed change mentioned previously in relation to the DSM classifications.

If we move away from the medical or health related perspective we find literature that takes a different view based on some of the work undertaken. An example of this is the work of Barton-Breck (2010) who in his research, indicates that the majority of his subjects stated that their self-injury was not associated with an illness, psychiatric or psychological condition. This further expands the debate of self-harm/injury and incorporates an activity that does not necessarily subscribe to the 'clinical' model of identification, at least not in the estimation of many of those individuals who participated in this study.

Another important consideration associated with self-harming/injuring activity is that of cultural diversity. It is pertinent to note that different cultures and societies have differing views on a range of activities. What is deemed 'normal' or 'acceptable' is one may not be in another. Examples such as ritualized scarification occur in some groups (e.g. Betamarribe people in Benin in West Africa, the Sambia people of Papua New Guinea) and these are seen as an integral and important part of the individual's journey towards adulthood. This has also resulted in reluctance on the part of some anthropologists to use the term of self-mutilation introduced by Favazza in the 1980's and early 1990's, instead opting for the use of the term body modification.

An article by Zislin et al (2002) adds a degree of contention in its exploration of the existence of self-mutilation 'sanctioned' by religious belief. What is apparent from these examples is that a range of practices although sanctioned by a part, if not all of the population in some parts of the world or society would be deemed totally unacceptable if they occurred somewhere else.

If we turn to the large range of information both published and available online on the topic it is again apparent that there is a marked diversity in the interpretation of what self-harm/injury is and the language used to explain it. The following are a range of explanations and definitions from both published literature and online information. It is neither intended to reflect all of the views that are currently held or an accepted range of these but to indicate the diversity of interpretations present.

1. **Books, reports, and articles**:

- In a 1998 publication Conterio and Lader indicated that it 'represents a frantic attempt by someone with low coping skills to "mother herself" '(p20)
- NICE (2004) define self-harm as 'an expression of personal distress usually made in private, by an individual who hurts her or himself' (p16)
- Sutton (2005) regards it as a 'compulsion or impulse to inflict physical wounds' (p2)
- The word mutilation mentioned above has largely been removed in more recent material and Walsh (2008) indicates it is about intentional bodily harm.
- Ousey and Ousey (2010) simply state at the beginning of their article that self-harm 'is a behaviour, not an illness'.

- Ougrin et al (2010) have dedicated an entire chapter in their book in an attempt to define the topic but have concluded that self-harm relates to a wide range of behaviours and have retained the NICE definition (mentioned above) for their particular publication.
- A report by the Royal College of Psychiatrists (2010) offers some interesting variations and stated differences in the appendix of the report regarding definitions and concepts of self-harm. The following two are offered as an example:
- 'Self-harm is a symptom not a disorder itself. Where self-harm exists as part of a mental illness, then the illness should be treated. Where there is no mental illness then this is not any business of psychiatry or psychiatrists. We do harm by medicalising the stress of everyday life and holding out a utopian view of happiness for all.' (ID 821)
- 'Your definition of self-harm is rather too broad to be…useful in elderly psychiatry, when there are so many ways people with dementia can cause themselves harm.' (ID 1165)

2. Internet based information:

- FirstSigns on their website identify it as a way of coping through physical harm to enable the individual to either deal with 'emotional pain' or to 'arouse sensations'.
- The Royal College of Psychiatrists again use a brief explanation: 'self-harm happens when someone hurts or harms themselves'.
- Moran and Borschmann (2011) indicates that: 'the term 'self-harm' refers to a wide range of intentional behaviors that cause damage, mutilation or destruction of the body without suicidal intent'

- Self-harm can take many different forms and as an individual act is hard to define. However in general self-harm (also known as self-injury or self-mutilation) is the act of deliberately causing harm to oneself either by causing a physical injury, by putting oneself in dangerous situations and/or self-neglect. [www.nshn.co.uk] [National Network for Self-Harm]

- Self-injury can be many things that people do to themselves in a deliberate and often hidden way like cutting, burning, overdosing, scratching, biting, hair pulling and breaking bones. [www.selfinjurysupport.org.uk] [Bristol Crisis Service for Women]

- Self-harm involves injury or harm with a non-fatal outcome as a way of coping with unbearable feelings. [www.samaritans.org] [The Samaritans]

- Self-harm is when someone deliberately hurts, cuts or injures him/herself. [spunout.ie] [Spunout Ireland]

- The S.A.F.E. ALTERNATIVES® philosophy begins with the assumption that, although temporarily helpful self-injurious behaviour is ultimately a dangerous and futile coping strategy which interferes with intimacy, productivity and happiness. There is no "safe" or "healthy" amount of self-injury. 'We also believe that self-injury is not an addiction over which one is powerless for a lifetime, people can and do stop injuring, with the right kinds of help and support. Self-injury can be transformed from a seemingly uncontrollable compulsion to a choice.' [www.selfinjury.com] [S.A.F.E. Alternatives]

- Self-injury - also called self-harm and self-abuse - refers to deliberate acts that cause harm to one's body, mind and spirit. [www.cmha.ca] [Canadian Mental Health Association]

- Deliberate self-harm (also known as self-injury) is when you deliberately inflict physical harm on yourself, usually in secret and often without anyone else knowing. [au.reachout.com] [REACH OUT.com – Australia]
- Self-harm (also known as deliberate self-injury or self-mutilation) is one way some young people use to cope with really difficult feelings - such as sadness, anger and worry - that build up inside and can get overwhelming. [www.headspace.org.nz] [Headspace – New Zealand]

As can be seen from much of the information provided on the previous couple of pages there is the regularly recurring theme that self-harm/injury generally refers to someone harming themselves in a variety of different ways, intentionally and to address issues linked to an emotional state. Hawton and Harriss (2008) in their article explore self-harm and suicide relationships across the life cycle. If we exclude the relationship debate regarding suicide what emerges is a suggestion that self-harming behaviour may vary in its intention both in life cycle and gender terms.

The detail relating to what the person actually does by way of physical harm/injury is usually absent from the initial statement and may sometimes be identified later in the information provided either in the published literature or in the web based information. This is an important point as it helps to remove the focus from what the person has physically done to the more important issues linked to why the behaviour may have occurred. This should help to reinforce the value of the primary issue as being one of listening to the person rather than addressing the physical need, although this should not be ignored.

One of the current stereotypes that exists is that people who self-harm/injure are young, female and attention seeking. This is unfortunately not helped by the fact that much of the general media has directed its focus at young people. This, to some extent may have been influenced by the fact that much of the published literature is in fact focused on young people. The profile stereotypically presented of a young person engaged in behaviour that seeks to attract attention has the unfortunate result of sometimes creating the impression of a rather simplistic interpretation of what is actually a very complex area. It also produces an inaccurate impression of who is involved overall in self-harming/injuring and why it is occurring.

It is also rather unfortunate that some older people hold the view that: 'in my day there was no such thing...' This view by an older person demonstrates that they have probably not been aware that some of their peers may well have been self-harming/injuring but had not advertised the fact to anyone else as the topic received very little public and professional attention until relatively recently. This has an important impact on young people who do self-harm/injure as some of these 'older' people will be their parents or professionals who they access and the limited understanding will have implications for all concerned.

Much of the material currently published in professional journals and books has a much broader base but is frequently aimed at professional groups, either engaged in training for their qualifications or as part of continuing professional development after qualification. The literature may focus on research undertaken in an attempt to identify any number of aspects, including:

- Incidence of self-harm/injury in a particular population
- Comparisons related to people presenting to areas like accident and emergency departments (e.g. type of harm/injury, gender)

- Relationship/link with suicide/mental illness
- Role of the professional in a self-harm/injury context
- Types of intervention (e.g. psychosocial interventions such as cognitive behavioural therapy)

In addition to this literature found in professional journals, other material on the same area may attempt to explore different elements that have specific meaning for both health professionals and individuals who self-harm/injure and have engaged with those very professionals. The result of this encounter is now more frequently explored, including:

- Experience of individuals presenting to areas such as an accident and emergency department of a hospital in their interactions with practitioners
- Education and training and its impact on the interventions undertaken by practitioners
- The role of the individual who self-harms/injures in the education and training of practitioners and indeed in the formulation of policies and protocols that practitioners will utilise
- Alternatives to the range of professional intervention strategies already identified

The alternative to this is material that can frequently be found linked to an expanding support network outside of the mainstream professional arena that has steadily developed. This has many of its origins in the initiatives of individuals who through their experiences viewed that more could be achieved than was currently on offer. This led to them frequently developing small support groups. These were mostly developed as a direct result of the lack of local information, support and awareness of issues around the subject. The need to address this was the motivating factor and a belief that statutory agencies were not doing so or, if they were, were not considered to necessarily be doing an effective job.

With the emergence via technology of the Internet, the opportunity of not only reaching a local audience but of reaching others both nationally and internationally now existed. This led to a rapid expansion not only in the number of groups emerging but also in the sharing and comparing of information and resources that were being developed. An increase in the variety, quality and accessibility offered through this medium has led to ever increasing services including; links, advice, training, information leaflets, booklets, books, CDs, DVDs and blogs. Some of the groups who provide such material are mentioned in the contact section later in the book.

Alas, along with the advent of modern technology came the opportunity not only of communicating something that was of value but in ultimately offering a forum where literally anyone could say and present anything. This then introduces the need for a degree of caution to be exercised when searching through this vast amount of information now currently available. Information varies from the somewhat questionable in terms of its content accuracy and value to detailed information that is of value to any number of potential individuals and/or groups.

In an attempt to reflect some of the range of information that is now currently available through a vast array of different mediums the next section identifies and offers, by way of examples, some of that currently on offer. The information that is made available here is presented to reflect the dichotomy that exists without necessarily advocating it as truly representative of all that there is. To aid with identification headings are used to signify the type of material offered.

Research

A vast repository of research-based material is now available and may be provided in report, article, book and guidance formats. Some examples of such documents that are currently readily available to anyone who wishes to explore the subject further include the following:

a. Reports; Guidance:

Self-harm: The short-term physical and psychological management and secondary prevention of self-harm in primary and secondary care. (2004)

This document issued guidance primarily to those either accessing or working within the NHS. It outlined an interpretation of self-harm and attempted to clarify distinctions within what were considered different perspectives and issues of self-harming (e.g. an attempt to end life, linked to dissociative states). The outcome was an attempt to bring a degree of consensus on what constituted self-harm and how individuals who self-harmed should be accommodated by practitioners in 'a therapeutic alliance.' This acknowledged that practice could and should improve when it came to how people who self-harmed/injured should be treated in the future.

Truth Hurts (2006)

This report identified its primary focus as young people, with a central part of its work issues relating to; incidence rates, support issues and an understanding of what self-harm was. The report was the culmination of a two-year study and contains a wealth of information, including indications of what individuals thought would be of help, albeit with an orientation towards young people only.

Understanding self-harm (2008)

This report was produced in part as an ongoing work (having commenced in 2005 through the use of a web based questionnaire) and contains prompts in bold that encourage the reader to contact and comment on specific points and constructs. It reports on a survey that attracted almost 1000 people. It is intended for a diverse audience and indicates that its intention is, in part, that of 'a source of information.... a discussion point.' It is also one of the few published pieces of work that acknowledge that not all self-harm/injury is related to young people, as the age range of participants (who were still self-harming) was 12-59.

Youth and self-harm: Perspectives (2009)

This report again has a focus on young people, but within the 15-16 year-old age range and conducted within a school-based environment (41 schools in total). It was however not specifically restricted to self-harm as the report indicates that the evidence is a study 'of deliberate self-harm and suicidal thought' (p7) within the stated population sample involved.

Self-harm, suicide and risk: helping people who self-harm (2010)

This report is divided into three primary sections and culminates in the exploration of a range of views and experiences derived from service users, staff surveys, and research. It does not specify any discrete group by age or gender but instead balances a reported improvement in practice with the recognition that there is still ongoing work to address some less desirable practice in what are described as 'clear indications of fault lines.'(p8)

b. Books:

Contemplating Suicide: The language of Ethics and Self-Harm (1995)

This book explored terminological issues and in part that of suicide (act of deliberately killing oneself) and parasuicide (acts that resemble suicide but the individual does not die). The construct of 'suicidal self-harm' is included but importantly the author indicates: 'the way we think about self-harm will be affected by the expectations to which the labels we use refer to self-harming acts, give rise' (p48).

The Language of Injury: Comprehending Self-Mutilation (1998)

This book identified as its primary objective a hope that it might: 'enable practitioners through awareness, to feel less helpless, overwhelmed, distressed and infuriated by self-injury...'(p ix) Much of the discussion revolved around the concept of self-injury and it was defined as: 'one part of a large repertoire of behaviours that involve the body in the expression of distress within the individual' (p2).

Hidden Self-Harm: Narratives from Psychotherapy (2003)

This book explores the concept of self-harm from a different perspective and engages the reader in a more circumspect way. There is a move away from the medicalization idea and instead one illuminating statement early in the book summarises the approach: 'In introducing the idea of 'casha' and examining points of connection between 'normal' and 'abnormal' self-harming behaviour, the book offers an unusual framework for thinking about self-harm...Self-harm is viewed in the context of ordinary behaviour, rather than as a circumscribed difficulty or disorder.' (pp 20-21)

Culture and self-Harm: Attempted Suicide in South Asians in London *(2004)*

This book explores a specific population within this country. However, one definition that emerges later in the book tends to increase the suicide/self-harm confusion that exists in some of the literature rather than attempt to aid clarity as follows: 'Deliberate self-harm was defined as suicidal gestures and attempts to kill oneself – with any act of nonfatal outcome that attempts to cause or actually causes self-harm, or which would have done so without the intervention of others' (p166).

Self-Harm in Young People: A Therapeutic Assessment Manual (2010)

This book continues on a similar theme to the previous others by indicating that any attempt to clearly define/explain self-harm is a highly complex undertaking but indicates one proposal where the categorisation of 'deliberate self-injury syndrome' has emerged with no suicidal intent, feelings of tension and sense of relief after self-harm. One chapter of note explores hopes and expectations and concludes with: 'it may be of particular importance to focus on and address the young people's hopes and expectations in order to facilitate engagement and aftercare' (p115)

The Art and Science of Mental Health Nursing (2nd Edition) (2009)

This book, though not specifically with a focus on self-harm/injury has been included as an example of change in terms of concepts and areas of knowledge and practice deemed essential for the modern mental health nurse. In this book there is an entire chapter dedicated to working with people who 'self-harm or are suicidal' (Chapter 34). Although both issues are again explored together this is generally the case amongst much of the professional literature available and can even be noted in the more specialist texts already mentioned.

c. **Journals**:

The following is a list of journals in which self-harm/injury articles have been published indicating the attempts that have been made to inform, educate and advise an ever-expanding body of practitioners on this subject. It is not a complete list of all journals but as mentioned with previous resources, an introduction to the spectrum of what is available.

- Accident and Emergency Nursing
- American Journal of Psychiatry
- British Journal of Clinical Psychology
- British Journal of General Practice
- British Journal of Learning Disabilities
- British Journal of Psychiatry
- British Medical Journal
- Clinical Child Psychology and Psychiatry
- Counselling and Psychology Quarterly
- Counselling and Psychotherapy Research
- Disability and Society
- Emergency Nurse
- Health Education
- Healthcare Counselling and Psychotherapy Journal
- Journal of Adolescence
- Journal of Clinical Nursing
- Journal of Advanced Nursing
- Journal of Forensic Psychiatry and Psychology
- Journal of Learning Disabilities and Offending behaviour
- Journal of Psychiatric and Mental Health Nursing
- Journal of Social Work
- Journal of Youth and Adolescence

- Learning in Health and Social Care
- Medicine
- Mental Health Practice
- Mental Health Review Journal
- Pastoral Care in Education
- Practice Nurse
- Psychoanalytic Psychotherapy
- Public Health Nursing
- Sociology of Health and Illness

Another aspect that deserves a mention is the recognition in literature and elsewhere of the value of information that can be derived from the internet. This is an important development as previously this source was viewed with some scepticism by many professionals and perceived as at best of limited value and at worst positively dangerous. Although this is still the case to some extent, there is now recognition that most young people have access to and actively use this medium for a variety of different purposes. If the subject area is to be effectively explored then this medium cannot be overlooked for the potential that exists. Some of the 'mentions' are identified in the material offered in the following examples in historical terms (earliest mention first):

- Prasad and Owens (2001) – this article looked at information found on the internet and identified the potential value associated with it. They stated in their discussion that 'professionals involved with people who self-harm would benefit from knowing something about the kind of material available to those who visit websites' and that they need 'to understand more clearly than they do at present how helpful, disconcerting or harmful people find the sites'. (p223-4)

- Bywaters and Rolfe (2002) – a variety of sources of help are identified at the end of the report together with the following: 'Please note that there are many other internet web-sites which cover self-harm. The content and quality of these is very varied. Take care about what you see and read' (p43).

- Mental Health Foundation (2006) – 'websites and internet forums have become increasingly popular with young people as a way to access information and support (p27).

- Whitlock et al (2007) – 'mental health professionals who are less familiar with the changes in the Internet would be well advised to educate themselves about the Web-based modalities available to their clients' (p1140)

- Royal College of Psychiatrists (2010) – In their leaflet called Self-Harm one of the 'Dos' identified is 'take some of the mystery out of self-harm by helping them find out about self-harm perhaps by showing them this leaflet, or by using the internet or local library'

- UKCCIS (2010) - The United Kingdom Council for Child Internet Safety in its updated good practice guide mentions self-harm as one aspect of 'social networking and user-interactive services'. It takes a balanced view indicating that 'to the extent that it allows them to express their feelings and seek support, this can be a positive experience' but 'there can be negative or worrying aspects of this exploration and engagement which can manifest themselves in the   apparent promotion or encouragement of self-harm' (p15).

One publication that I encountered was rather surprising in its use of terminology given the publication date. In a literature review McDonald et al (2009) explored deviant behaviour and the impact of the internet. It is of interest given the previous look at information derived from both published sources and the internet. One of the three groups identified within the article was a self-harm group. In their abstract they indicated that they were attempting to 'enhance our understanding of the role(s) that the Internet plays in supporting or encouraging deviant behaviors.'

It would appear unfortunate that terminology such as 'deviant' is still being applied at this point in time. In using the term it is unlikely to instil any motivation on the part of someone who is self-harming/injuring to seek support, help and/or advice due to the potential stigma already apparent.

Summary

It is now apparent that there is a range of different interpretations of what self-harm/injury is or may be. It is somewhat complicated by the wide range of terms utilised to identify it. These, in turn, occasionally introduce associations and links with concepts such as suicide and mental illness and in one case deviancy that in turn do little to aid clarity to the overall picture. It may be prudent to consider that it may be of value to listen to what the individual who self-harms/injures says. Each individual's experience will be unique and it is not something that - like a light bulb - can be readily switched on or off. If we consider this we may then be in a better position to understand and in turn support the individual more effectively than is happening at present. Things are improving but as is frequently stated they 'could be better'.

References:

American Psychiatric Association (1994) The Diagnostic and Statistical manual of mental Disorders (DSM-IV)

Babiker G & Arnold L (1998) *The Language of Injury: Comprehending Self-Mutilation*, Leicester, British Psychological Society

Barton-Breck AJT (2010) *The development of self-injury as a multi-functional behaviour*, PhD Thesis, University of Greenwich

Bhugra D (2004) *Culture and Self-Harm: Attempted Suicide in South Asians in London*, Hove, Psychology Press

Bywaters P & Rolfe A (2002) *Looking beyond the scars: Understanding and responding to self-injury and self-harm*, London, NCH

Chandler A, Myers F, Platt S (2011) The Construction of Self-Injury in the Clinical Literature: A Sociological Exploration, *Suicide and Life-Threatening Behavior*, Volume 41, issue 1, pp98-109

Conterio K & Lader W (1998), *Bodily Harm*, New York, Hyperion, p20

Fairburn GJ (1995) *Contemplating Suicide: The Language of Ethics and Self-Harm, London*, Routledge

Favazza AR (1996) *Bodies under siege: Self-mutilation and body modification in culture and psychiatry* (2nd ed), Baltimore, John Hopkins University Press

FirstSigns, *What self-injury is*, www.firstsigns.org.uk/what/

Hawton K, Harriss L (2008) How Often Does Deliberate Self-Harm Occur Relative to Each Suicide? A Study of variations by Gender and Age, *Suicide and Life-Threatening Behaviour*, Volume 38, Issue 6, pp650-660

Horne O & Paul S (2008) *Understanding self-harm*, SANE

McDonald HS, Horstmann N, Strom KJ, Pope MW (2009) *The Impact of the Internet on Deviant Behavior and Deviant Communities*, Institute for Homeland Securities Solutions

Mental Health Foundation (2006) *Truth Hurts: Report of the National Inquiry into Self-harm among Young People*

Moran P, Borschmann R (2011) *Self-harm*, www.pulsetoday.co.uk/

NCCMH (2004) *Self-harm: The short-term physical and psychological management and secondary prevention of self-harm in primary and secondary care*

NCCMH (April 2011) *Self-harm: longer-term management in adults, children and young people, Draft* for consultation

NICE (2004) *Self-harm: The short-term physical and psychological management and secondary prevention of self-harm in primary and secondary care*, London, National Institute for Clinical Excellence

Norman I, Ryrie I (2009) The Art and Science of Mental Health Nursing (2nd Edition), Maidenhead, Open University Press

Ougrin D, Zundel T, Ng AV (2010) *Self-harm in Young People: A therapeutic assessment manual*, London, Hodder Arnold

Ousey K, Ousey C (2010) Intervention strategy for people who self-harm, *Wounds UK*, Volume 6, Number 4, pp34-40

Prasad V, Owens D (2001) Using the internet as a source of help for young people who self-harm, *Psychiatric Bulletin*, 25, pp222-225

Royal College of Psychiatrists, *Self-Harm leaflet*, www.rcpsych.ac.uk/mentalhealthinfoforall/problems/depression/self-harm.aspx

Royal College of Psychiatrists (2010), *Self-harm, suicide and risk: helping people who self-harm: Final report of a working group*, 119-120

Samaritans & Centre for Suicide Research, University of Oxford (2009) *Youth and self-harm: Perspectives – A report*, Samaritans

Sansone RA, Lam C, Wiederman MW (2009) Self-Harm Behaviors Among Internal Medicine Outpatients, *The Journal of Medicine*, Volume 2, Number 5, pp241-243

Sinclair J, Green J (2005) Understanding resolution of deliberate self-harm: qualitative interview study of patients' experiences, BMJ, doi:10.1136/bmj.38441.503333.8F, available at http://www.bmj.com/content/330/7500/1112.full.pdf

Sutton J (2005), *Healing the hurt within*, Oxford, Howtobooks, p2

Turp M (2003) *Hidden Self-Harm: Narratives from Psychotherapy*, London, Jessica Kingsley Publishers Ltd.

UKCCIS (2010) *Good Practice guidance for the providers of social networking and other user-interactive services*

Walsh BW (2008), *Treating Self-Injury: A Practical Guide*, London, The Guildford Press

Watts N (2011) Self Harm & Negative Coping Strategy Breaking the Cycle, http://www.healthyhappieryou.co.uk/2011/03/self-harm-negative-coping-strategy-breaking-the-cycle/

Whitlock J, Lader W, Conterio K (2007) The Internet and Self-Injury: What Psychotherapists Should Know, *Journal of Clinical Psychology: In Session*, Volume 63, Number 11, pp1135-1143

World Health Organisation (2007) International Statistical Classification of Diseases and Health related Problems (ICD-10)

Zislin J, Katz G, Raskin S, Strauss Z, Tettelbaum A & Durst R (2002) Male Genital Self-Mutilation in the Context of Religious belief: The Jerusalem Syndrome, *Transcultural Psychiatry*, Volume39, Number 2, pp257-264

A [age 40]

My name is A and I'm 40 years old. I'm in my second marriage and have a 17 year-old son from my first marriage. He is a very balanced, respectful and respectable young man. I was born in England, where I still live - having never moved away from the town where I was born. I have been employed by the NHS for 10 years, doing a variety of administrative roles.

My father had a mining accident when I was 10 that left him unable to work so my mother took on cleaning jobs to top up the little income they had from benefits.

I always seem to remember my parents didn't have the best of marriages and my father was very prone to outbursts of anger, periods of silence or a combination of both. I have one brother, who is 3 years older, who was very close with our mother. I felt like a burden to my parents and, looking back, I became very depressed around the age of 13.

My father was very critical of me. I never felt loved nor was I given any praise. Everyone outside the 'family home' thought he was a lovely man although my parents had barely any social life and very few friends. He ruled with dictation, fear, threats and criticism. Anytime I returned to the 'family home', I used to feel physically sick and my throat would close over, always wondering what mood I would encounter once I stepped through the door. I was rather underweight and underdeveloped because I didn't feel that I could eat.

My mother often told me she was happy with just my brother but I was born because my father wanted another child. She always said she was happy that she had a little girl though. I've never been able to make sense of that statement but can only surmise that I'd hate to have been a boy. She also used to tell me I should never have children. She made this statement based on the fact that I never played with dolls, choosing to read, write or get her to write me down lots of sums to do.

I always felt like an outsider. My brother had my mother. My mother had my father - in some bizarre way - and I had nobody. I also thought myself to be very bad. After all my brother was a naughty child and even if he got smacked he and my mother would always make up with apologies and cuddles. I was very compliant and would remove myself from any situation where, potentially, I may get smacked before it got to boiling point. I tried so hard to be good but still got little in the way of cuddles or praise.

I started to self-harm around the age of 14, using my maths compass to puncture my lower forearms. It looked like an allergy rash so I could use that as an excuse to hide it. I was also rather underdeveloped. When I cut it would release all the anxiety. I used it as a substitute for tears because if I cried it would show in my eyes and would lead to questions from my parents and possibly, teachers.

When I wasn't doing homework or music practice I would shut myself away in my room, cut, sleep or listen to music and read whilst drinking any alcohol I could find. I was simply accused of being moody. Nobody sat down to ask me what was going on because I wasn't ever really noticed.

Academically I was quite bright and also had a big interest in music, playing flute and piano. From around the age of 10 I had wanted to be a music teacher. Because of how things were at 'home' my schoolwork took a dive early in year 10, as I just couldn't cope with the pressure of things at home. I was given extra lessons in maths, chemistry and physics, which generated more homework on top of an already heavy load from school. I used to do 2 hours of music practice after I completed my homework on a daily basis. If I ever took an evening off to go out with friends I would have to make the practice up over other days. I had wanted to do woodwork at O' level but my parents didn't allow it because it wasn't an academic subject. The most relaxing lesson I was allowed to do was typing.

When I announced to my maths teacher, that I wouldn't be returning for sixth form to do 'A' levels he was shocked and contacted my parents to ask what was going on. He was the only person that believed in me. I felt very worthless and incapable of achieving anything. I was never going to be good enough so I decided the best thing for me was to get a job so I could earn and leave home as soon as possible. Of course, my mother until her dying day was convinced that I was having some kind of sexual relationship with my maths teacher. She dared to bring down his professionalism, integrity and simple care.

Once I started work at the age of 16 the cutting reduced, although eating was still an issue. I got engaged to my first husband at 17, five months after our first date and signed up for my first joint mortgage at the age of 18. Once I left home to live with my fiancé my eating improved and the cutting stopped altogether.

I gave birth to my son at the age of 23. I immediately became depressed again and felt useless as a mother and was frightened to be alone with him. I looked to my parents and in-laws for support. Again, my parents ruled how I cared for my son. My mother told me I shouldn't pick him up and cuddle him because he would become sore if handled too much. The only time my son really slept was when he was left with my mother in law who was wonderfully relaxed with him. My husband also told me how to care for our son and because I was compliant I would do as I was told.

My health visitor went on maternity leave and her replacement didn't identify post-natal depression. She told me I should spend less time with my parents. When my son was 2 and 1/2 my original health visitor returned and encouraged me to go to the doctor. I was put onto medication and had 6 sessions with a psychiatric nurse who visited me at home. Her main course of treatment was cognitive behavioural therapy (CBT).

I started to improve and stand up to my father by walking out, rather than stay and tolerate his poor behaviour. I thought he was the root of all my problems. One evening my husband and I were watching 'Casualty' which showed a scene of a woman who self harmed. I told him that I had done the same in the past. He gave little reaction.

I remember my mother throwing a huge criticism at me around the age of 26/27. I immediately turned to cutting but used safety razors instead. I was also very overweight at around a size 20. Her criticism upset me so much I could hardly eat for around 5 days. I told myself if I could do it for that length of time I could do it for always and started to lose weight by reducing my food intake drastically. Along with that came some confidence.

By the time I was 29 my first marriage had broken down. My mother was begging me to eat and I dropped to a size 6-8. I continued to cut. A year later, in 2000, my present husband moved in with me. I had mentioned my self-harm to him and he also didn't have much to say about it. I told him it would stop from then on.

My mother died of cancer in 2001 and I became my father's main carer. I felt happy in my life and thought that was how life would be. In 2006 I found my father dead and had a breakdown the following summer 2007. I kind of recovered and came off medication again in Jan 2009.

In May of that year I looked at the front page of a free local newspaper that was posted through the letterbox. It showed a photo of a man I knew from my childhood. He was a scoutmaster and had been convicted as a paedophile. I started getting flashbacks to something that had happened when I was 8 that was buried in the depths of my memory. All the feelings of guilt and shame came with it.

By November I was struggling to deal with it all thinking I was a perpetrator. I started to cut again using blades that are used in a pedicure implement. I cut on my forearms and thighs so I could cover up with long sleeves and trousers. The familiar sick feeling had also returned.

I went back to my GP at the beginning of December who put me on medication again. I was given the usual questionnaire to complete which is used as a guide to measure my level of depression. I wasn't spoken to about anything that I had scored including the feelings of suicide and wanting to hurt myself.

One evening in February of this year I was browsing Facebook and entered 'Self Harm' in the search field. There was an open group and I read the postings that had been put on. I didn't feel like a freak anymore. I didn't want to join the group for fear of being found out. Instead I contacted a member, via e-mail, who looked a similar age. Her postings made complete sense to me. I don't know how I found the strength to reach out to her but I didn't want to be alone anymore.

We were in touch every day. It was refreshing to be able to talk to someone who completely understood my feelings. After about a month I told her what had happened when I was 8 years old. I told her about how I had been left alone with a group of scouts in their early teens and the things they had got me to join in which they made seem fun. One of those boys was my brother. I talked with her about how he had told on me when he was in trouble as a way to take the attention of our mother away from him. The response I had from my parents and the other scout leader who 'interviewed' me left me feeling bad, guilty and ashamed. I had been interviewed whilst I was made to eat my dinner. From that point on I knew I was alone. I never really did feel I belonged to my family.

I was so shocked when my newfound friend told me minors had sexually abused me. I was already cutting every day and it increased to at least twice a day. I carried this knowledge around for a week in total shock and disbelief. I just wanted to die. I told my husband I had been sexually abused. He took me to the doctor the next day and I was referred to the mental health team for an emergency assessment.

I told the CPN about my cutting and eating problems but nothing was really made of it. I was discharged that day, as I wasn't seen as a threat to myself. She did say she didn't think I was on the right medication but would write to my GP and in the meantime double what I was on. She did put me in touch with the local NHS rape and sexual abuse centre. They put me on the list for therapy but there was a 6-month waiting list. They also offered me the choice of attending a support group for women who had suffered sexual abuse. I took up that offer.

I spoke to my GP about changing my medication but she refused. I asked her whether she knew of a good private therapist but she didn't and advised me against sourcing someone myself.

The co-ordinator of the support group got in touch and recommended one to one therapy and I told her I had 'hit a wall' with it all. Because I attended the group the co-ordinator was able to get me prioritised on the waiting list and I was allocated a therapist a couple of weeks later.

I have told my therapist about my self-harm but we've not discussed it in depth. The therapy has helped me to give ownership of the all abuse I suffered from those boys, my parents and my brother back to them. I have severed all communication and ties with all of my blood family. They were simply people I was born to. That's all. They're not people who I would choose as friends so why should I accept them otherwise? The feelings of the need to cut have reduced and I have achieved not cutting for 16 days so far. I slip from time to time but it's a whole lot better and there's no reason why it can't get better still with a lot more work on my self-care and self-worth.

My friend and I know we are to call each other if we feel the need to self-harm, as an alternative and she remains the only person on a personal level who is aware of my coping mechanisms.

I don't feel shame or guilt anymore for cutting but I just know that others won't understand which I why I do it. I just don't want to be judged any longer or made to feel bad for doing whatever it takes for me to survive. Surely self-harm is better than becoming overwhelmed to the point of suicide.

C [age 25]

My first experience of self-harm was when I was about 8 years old. I had suffered with depression, although this went undiagnosed until I was 19, and the frustration I felt was so overwhelming I didn't know what to do with myself. I remember sitting in my room crying, until the frustration I felt burst out of me and I started to yank my hair out in chunks. This continued until I reached 13.

At the age of 13 I discovered cutting. I would lock myself in the bathroom and pull apart the plastic disposable razors to release the razor blades. The first time I slid the razor blade across my thigh, I felt at peace. It was like the storm that was raging inside my head had suddenly stopped, all was calm. After the first time, it was like an addiction. Every time I felt emotional I would reach for the razor blades hidden in my room. I even took them to school just in case things became too difficult. No one knew what I was doing, I kept my thighs covered and I would skip P.E. if I had recently cut myself.

Throughout my teens, I self-harmed weekly and also developed an eating disorder. I was filled with hatred for myself with a rage that was frightening. I had my first boyfriend at 16 and the emotional rollercoaster continued with the added complexity of intimacy. He didn't seem too bothered by my scars or cuts, but I knew he didn't really understand it either. I had a suicide attempt when I was 17 after suffering a miscarriage but was not treated for either. My boyfriend and I split up when I was 18 and I met someone else within two weeks. With this new relationship, I began to feel something I had never felt before, security. I still self-harmed, but it was not as regular as before.

My new partner & I moved in together and just 11 months after we met, I was pregnant with our first child. After getting used to the idea, I was happy, but my partner distanced himself from me and my bump as the reality of having a baby was a difficult concept. The pregnancy was difficult and I developed antenatal depression, which developed into postnatal depression after the difficult birth of our son in December 2004. The self-harm started a few weeks after the birth, with me mainly pulling my hair out as I sat up all night feeding my son. I eventually had to stop breastfeeding in order to start taking antidepressant medication as I became suicidal. The medication helped and I started a full-time job when our son was just 4 months old. My partner became a stay-at-home dad while I worked and this suited our little family. This was the first time I could actually say that I was happy.

In August 2006, my partner, now my husband, and I decided to start trying for another baby and I fell pregnant immediately. This time I was determined to take control of my pregnancy and birth, which ran smoothly. I was still on antidepressant medication throughout the pregnancy, but taking the medication outweighed the possibility of my falling ill again during the pregnancy. I gave birth to our daughter at home in June 2007. However, I became depressed again when our daughter was 2 months old and was hospitalised for 10 days.

The self-harm began to increase when our daughter started going to our childminder at 6 months old, and I had started a new job. I was being bullied at work, my mental health was deteriorating and my relationship with my husband began to come apart at the seams. I had suffered episodes of dissociation and psychosis since childhood and these episodes became increasingly worse after I suffered repeated sexual abuse and rape at the age of 13. I could never explain these episodes to anyone at the time as I was worried people would think I was mad. During these episodes, I would self-harm to 'bring myself back'. Seeing the blood and feeling the pain made me realise I was 'real'.

Cleaning the wounds and bandaging them also helped me to comfort myself, this felt even stronger when my husband would help me too. I would feel loved and calm.

As my mental health became worse, I was having frequent suicide attempts and temper tantrums as I couldn't control the rage inside me. I was eventually diagnosed as having Borderline Personality Disorder (BPD) in early 2009 and was referred to a specialist program to help people with personality disorders. However, this was overshadowed by my relationship breakdown, especially after I was raped by 2 men in June 2009. The police did all they could but no charges were ever brought due to lack of evidence. My mood swings, self-harm and erratic behaviour caused my family such grief that my husband eventually asked me to leave in October 2009. This caused severe distress to me and after I found out my husband was seeing another woman, I tried to commit suicide again in February 2010. This time, I was nearly successful. I cut my arms up so bad that I had to see a plastics specialist at another hospital as I nearly severed the nerves in my wrist. The period between October 2009 and February 2010 was probably the worst I had experienced. During this time I had had 9 suicide attempts and my self-harm had escalated to shutting my leg in car doors, burning my arms, cutting my face, my neck and my genitals as well as the 'usual' places I cut.

After my hospitalisation in February, I knew I couldn't continue this way. For the sake of my children at least, I had to do something to change. I stopped drinking alcohol, began taking my medication properly and eventually started group therapy for BPD in Spring 2010. I am making great progress. I write poetry to help me cope with feelings before they overwhelm me and use the skills that I am being taught in group therapy. I still have the odd relapse, but am extremely proud to say that I have self-harmed only once since my hospitalisation in February 2010. It is extremely hard to break the cycle of self-abuse, but with support from professionals, family and friends, it is possible.

WHY DO PEOPLE SELF-HARM / INJURE?

The aim of this section is to explore some of the many reasons provided by people and literature for why people may engage in self-harm/injury. This emerges from both literature that has been explored and from conversations with individuals. It is worth mentioning that not everyone who self-harms/injures can readily and/or easily identify a reason for this. For those who do the reasons offered are many and varied and may even change in terms of what the individual does (in terms of self-harm/injury) in different emotional contexts (e.g. anxious or angry).

If we are to develop a greater understanding of this aspect of self-harm/injury then it is important that we provide an environment that is both physically and emotionally supportive and accommodating to encourage more people to come forward and share with others their specific experiences and associated reasons.

If an answer to the above readily existed, then much of what is being explored now would be pointless as we would already have the answer! It is therefore apparent that there are a multitude of reasons that people will provide in an effort to explain, not only to other people, but to themselves, why they self-harm/injure. It is also worth noting that not everyone has a clear understanding of why they need to self-harm/injure other than an urge or necessity indicating this course of action needs to be undertaken at some point.

Throughout the literature, there are attempts to explain reasons why people may self-harm/injure. By way of an introduction to this section, I have listed some of the range of responses that I have been provided with when talking with individuals who have themselves self-harmed/injured. The following are examples of some reasons provided that arose on a number of occasions and were indicated by the individuals as their consideration of why they were/had been self-harming/injuring.

They included:
- To feel
- To find relief
- To 'fit in'
- To express my distress
- To cope
- To prove I am alive
- To retain some control
- To express my anger

It is apparent from the small sample offered above that the reasons identified by individuals may be many and varied and may change between both individuals and situations.

The association or link with mental illness and self-harm/injury is another variable that frequently arises in the literature and is an important consideration but requires caution as not everyone who self-harms/injures has a mental illness. The implications of this will be addressed later in the book (i.e. Chapter 6 – looking at Interventions).

By way of comparison to the list presented above a number of other lists that have appeared in a range of literature and online have been identified and are introduced on the following pages. One example from abroad has been selected as a reminder that self-harm/injury is not an exclusive UK issue but one that affects many people in many countries. A New Zealand site for young people [www.headspace.org.nz] indicates that there are lots of different reasons why individuals may self-harm/injure but offer the following as examples:

- To release tension or angry feelings

- To distract themselves from emotional pain
- To snap out of dissociation
- To feel "real"
- To stop having a panic attack
- To stop lashing out at others
- To escape problems by getting "out of it"
- Self-hatred

[www.headspace.org.nz/young-people/self-harming.htm]

Barton-Breck (2010) in his research based in England identifies a range of factors. Some are already replicated in lists previously utilised but it is important that this does not detract from the variations that are introduced. He indicates a range of these factors and indicates these are some but not all of those that were identified. They included:

- Social factors (e.g. difficulties in interacting with others)
- Emotional factors (e.g. overwhelming emotional distress)
- Cognitive factors (e.g. negative thoughts and memories)
- Physiological factors (e.g. need to feel physical pain)
- Communication factors (e.g. being verbally discounted)
- Occupational factors (e.g. having difficulty in education or work)
- Behavioural factors (e.g. using different forms of self-injury)

Nock (2008, 2010) in a detailed analysis of potential factors related to self-harm/injury put forward, a four-function model indicating that the functions of self-harm/injury might be related to reinforcement that was either negative or positive and either related to an intrapersonal or interpersonal construct. Some examples of the thinking included:

1. Increase in desired feeling (e.g. self-stimulation) [+ intrapersonal]
2. Decrease in feelings (e.g. tension relief) [-intrapersonal]
3. Increase in a desired social event (e.g. attention, support) [+ interpersonal]
4. Decrease in some social event (e.g. bullying) [-interpersonal]

Martin et al (2010) in a unique major study undertaken in Australia identified that the two main reasons provided by those interviewed who had self-harmed/injured (both male and female) were to manage emotions and self-punishment. Lader (2006) in a thought-provoking article examining the way in which people modified their appearances in a multitude of different ways (including self-harm/injury) summarised by stating that: 'I believe that the increase in addictions, like body focused behaviors, can be attributed to the increase in the fragmentation of our society, as well as our families, where individuals experience themselves as just that, individual, separate, alienated people without a sense of structure, acceptance, love and belonging.'(p 18)

What is not in doubt is that the need to self-harm/injure is motivated by specific reasons that the individuals themselves may not even necessarily be aware of. This in turn leads to activity that may create an equally strong set of emotions within that person. A number of research projects have explored this   aspect, amongst many others, in an attempt to increase knowledge and understanding and to assist both the individual who self-harms/injures and practitioners who may be involved with that person at some stage in their journey through or within self-harm/injury.

As mentioned at the beginning of this section, a range of literature has been explored. Some of this with either a focus based on the specific identification of reasons for self-harming/injuring or content which incudes such information is introduced over the following few pages. This is compared to and contrasted with other sources including group projects, internet based information and the stories provided by individuals later in this book. It is important to explore a range of sources and then examine them in more detail to identify potential similarities, marked differences and any areas that offer some indication of the value that this information may have in terms of helping the individual who self-harms/injures.

Hospital attendances:

The NHS Information Centre (2011) indicated a rise over three years of nearly 10,000 (around 10%) in the number of people who were admitted having self-harmed/injured. One published piece that has been collating a large amount of information over a number of years is the University of Manchester's ongoing self-harm project (MASH). A number of reports and updates have been produced and in its latest report for 2008 a range of precipitating factors were highlighted that were associated with individuals and self-harming/injuring. It is apparent from a comparative viewpoint that similarities are shared with previous information earlier in this chapter.

It is however pertinent to not only examine the factors listed but their significance in relation to repetition in terms of the number of individuals who identified them. These factors identified within the document have been reproduced (with permission) in an adapted format in Figure 1. The elements are presented in ascending order with those most frequently cited by the participants presented last (i.e. number 1). The issues of gender is also identified and the '+' used in the diagram represents in which gender group (i.e. male or female) that specific factor was most frequently cited.

Although not identified within this particular version, the original model in the report established that; *number 1: relationship problem with partner* is significantly more prominent and nearly twice as frequently cited as the nearest other factor as a specific precipitant. This is pertinent as the actual sample group compromised of quite significant number, namely 2,375 people.

Figure 1: **Precipitants of self-harm for individuals** (Adapted from Dickson et al, 2011)

List	Factor	*M	*F
18	Miscarriage, stillbirth	No	Y
17	Victim of crime	Y	Y+
16	Legal problem	Y+	Y
15	Abuse	Y	Y+
14	Other	Y	Y
13	Bullying	Y	Y+
12	Substance abuse	Y+	Y
11	Physical health problem	Y	Y+
10	Bereavement	Y	Y+
9	Other mental health issues	Y	Y
8	Direct response to mental symptoms	Y+	Y
7	Housing problem	Y+	Y
6	Relationship problem with others	Y	Y+
5	Financial problem	Y+	Y
4	Employment or study problem	Y+	Y
3	Alcohol abuse	Y+	Y
2	Relationship problem with family	Y	Y+
1	Relationship problem with partner	Y+	Y

* M=Males; F=Females

The information displayed in Figure 1 once again highlights the diverse range of reasons and circumstances that may be associated with individuals and their 'need' to self-harm/injure.

O'Connor et al (2009) in their study based around Scottish schools and adolescents identified the following reasons provided by young people:

- To get relief from a terrible state of mind (74.5%)
- Wanting to punish oneself (51.9%)

A somewhat disconcerting finding that has emerged in articles by Young et al (2007) and O'Connor et al (2009) was the significant response in terms of the most frequently expressed reasons for self-harming expressed by young people involved in the surveys:

- Wanted to die – 37.6% [O'Connor et al]
- To kill myself – 18.9% males; 23.1% females [Young et al]

This again reintroduces the issues related to associations between self-harm and suicide or at least suicidal ideation (i.e. thinking about/expressing thoughts of wishing to die). Although the overall figures - particularly in the work of Young et al - are quite small (18.9% males = 7; 23.1% females = 12) they are nevertheless an indication that enabling the individual to talk is vital in establishing important information, even if we do not necessarily like what we are hearing! Another example of this (not liking what we hear) is in the early work of Lloyd (1990) who in a literature review on suicide and self-harm/injury in prisons indicated that the literature concluded (in relation to 'girls' who cut themselves) 'that girls who cut themselves once had realised that in order to gain acceptance they had to cut themselves – but they only need to do this once' (p27).

Wishart (2004) introduced another identified range of functions for self-harm in their report (see Figure 2).

Figure 2: Checklist for Identifying the Functions of Self-Harm

What is important to you about self-harming?

I need to feel pain	I need to feel punished
It helps me to feel sensation	It's how I ask for help
It helps me to stop feeling	It helps me forget
It's a channel for my rage	It helps distract me from memories
It lets me know I'm alive	It's a safe way to let myself feel
It helps me to stay alive	It's a way to express what's inside
It helps me to space out	It helps me cry
It helps me feel grounded	It's soothing and comforting
It releases tension	I can't remember why it's important
I know where I begin and end	I just feel like I'm supposed to
It's the only way I feel sexual	It helps me know my edges

It makes everything less real	It helps me know my edges
It's what I learned to do	It's a way to communicate
It's a way to communicate	I need to see the blood or the marks
It's familiar	It helps me to "go away"
I release my frustrations that way	Other
Other	Other

[Adapted from Connors RE (2000) Self-Injury: Psychotherapy with people who engage in self-inflicted violence. Northvale, NJ: J. Aronson in Wishart M (2004) Adolescent self-harm: An exploration of the Nature and Prevalence in Banyule/Nillumbik, Nillumbik Community Health Service]

Motz (2009) in exploring what self-harm/injury is about and to some extent why people may self-harm/injure states 'Self-harm can be understood as a way of saying through gestures and acts of violence, that which cannot be put in words' (p21).

As an introduction to the next element and by way of trying to integrate some of the many factors introduced previously, I have devised an acronym (Figure 3) that helps me to try and appreciate the key aspects of an episode of self-harm/injury. It aims to place what might be occurring in some degree of order in an attempt to understand more effectively the 'ingredients' that need to come together for an episode of self-harm/injury to be considered or to take place.

Each component is identified and related issues are introduced in an effort to clarify what the process might consist of.

Figure 3: **T.I.M.E.**

✓ **T** – the 'trigger' that creates an inclination to act. This is in terms of the feeling(s) that generates a thought and/or need related to self-harm/injury

✓ **I** - this describes the intensity, immediacy or impulsivity of/associated with the feeling(s) and to what degree it requires addressing (i.e. thought and/or action)

✓ **M** – the maintenance or management of control. This identifies the degree of potential safety or risk associated with the action

✓ **E** - end, exit, or emergence of/from the feeling(s). This identifies to what extent the feeling(s) have been resolved

---

It is important to note that in each of the elements identified, each individual may have different issues determining what the eventual outcome will be. The term 'trigger' here is utilised somewhat differently from its general application in relation to self-harm/injury. Here it relates to the issue, circumstance, feeling and/or need that initiate either thoughts or action linked to self-harm/injury. By way of an example, figure 4 explores two possible scenarios to clarify this. The factors that are seen to alter the 'balance' of the behaviour are those of impulsivity/intensity/immediacy and that of control (**I & M**). If the individual has embarked on self-harming/injuring with some clarity related to their welfare and/or safety the outcome is likely to enable that person to regain or retain control. If however the intensity of the trigger results in action which may not be subject to some degree of control the outcome may not be a resolution that reduces the situation in 'satisfactory' terms for the individual. A situation that introduces the need for external intervention (primarily health related) may result in an outcome that removes or compromises the ability of the individual to regain or retain control.

Figure 4: **Variations in a scenario of self-harm/injury outcome**

SCENARIO 1	SCENARIO 2
T = situation that initiates a need to feel(e.g. pain, punishment, release, relief)	**T** = situation that initiates a need to feel(e.g. pain, punishment, release, relief)
I = immediacy of the need (thought or action)	**I** = immediacy of the need (thought or action)
M = degree of control exercised in terms of what is taking place	**M** = control is compromised by necessity to act.
E = the need has been addressed through the action and resolved	**E** = the initial need has been resolved through the action but the outcome may introduce further need [due to the compromise introduced to the individual's immediate welfare]

Triggering:

All of the information within this section has until now, had as its focus a range of reasons derived primarily from the literature, internet and personal discussions. One additional issue that arises quite frequently is that of 'images'. This relates principally to the effects of visual information, usually in the form of pictures, photographs, videos and/or drawings depicting activity relating to self-harm/injury or its aftermath. Although the internet is still viewed with some ambivalence by many professionals it is undoubtedly a significant source of information, advice and support for many people who self-harm/injure, particularly young people.

Anyone who searches online for information that contains images, particularly in areas such as forums, message boards and indeed YouTube may encounter a cautionary front page or banner that indicates that some of the content may be 'triggering'. This indicates that individuals who are in a sensitive or vulnerable state may encounter images that could lead to the potential of them engaging in a self-harming/injuring activity as a result.

Even though for many people access to 'the web' has been available for at least two decades, its impact is still unclear. Webb et al (2008) in their article describing the introduction of the Reach Out forum in Australia indicate that their anecdotal information suggests that young people have found the resource a very positive and valuable experience. The bulletin board is facilitated by young people but in collaboration with trained monitors. They have indicated their disquiet that there are still however many unsupervised forums and chat rooms used by young people and that little evidence currently exists as to the value or otherwise of these. Mitchell and Ybarra (2007) stated in their work that although young people were more likely to incorporate risky behaviour in online situations, because of their frequent use of chat rooms and forums, programs aimed at helping young people should incorporate a chat room and instant messaging to their hotlines.

Norris (2007) cited a study that identified some 400 self-injury message boards mainly populated by young females. There was a suggestion that concern exists that 'there might be a risk of normalising and encouraging self-injurious behaviour' through these forums. A TIME Photos site explores self-injury in Japan through a photo gallery and this contains a number of quite graphic photos but also provides a clear message at the beginning before the 'enter' option is used.

It is difficult to determine whether what is being displayed is meant to educate, shock, or bring a hidden behaviour into the open to enable awareness and recognition of the topic. This could be seen as an attempt to recognise the existence of the behaviour but could equally be criticised for enabling anyone curious about the topic to access material, despite the warning, that could lead to the possibility of some individuals self-harming/injuring or of others deciding on an interpretation that is not representative of self-harming/injuring in its entirety.

Lewis et al (2011) searched YouTube for information related to self-harm/injury and concluded that of the top 100 videos analysed, most were   mainly factual or educational, most contained quite explicit imagery but less than half (42%) provided a triggering or advance warning about the explicit nature of the content.

In defence of the value that may come from careful and selective use of information and advice/support source on the internet it is pertinent to note that this is not the only source of concern. Pembroke (2005) in a guest editorial identified the media as an area of concern, particularly in relation to self-harm/injury. She stated that: 'this topic is especially vulnerable to the worst excesses of the media with encouragement of demands for pictures of people's scars.' (p1)

A recent BBC News article (2010) explored the issues of self-harm/injury as a result of noting that the admission rate to hospital in the UK of young people who had cut themselves had risen by 50%. It indicated that, although responsible material existed on the internet and forums where young people could share their feelings online were available, it was being compromised by other accessible material that had little moderation and in a few extreme instances actively supported, promoted and provided photo images of injuries.

It might help to introduce at this point an acknowledgement that 'even' in the professional literature images can exist that are included within a published piece of work and do not provide any advance notification or 'trigger' warning. One such example is a recent article by Myer (2011) that features quite graphic drawings within the article and yet no advance warning on the first page.

Summary:

This section has introduced a range of material that looks at some of the many reasons offered related to why people may self-harm/injury. These have been identified through a range of processes and include professional assessment, research studies and self-reporting. The myriad of reasons provided helps to explain the challenges that exist in attempting to identify patterns, people and places in an effort to understand this area more meaningfully. We are aware that self-harm/injury may be linked statistically to certain groups and cultures but more importantly can occur irrespective of culture, age, gender or circumstance. A model (T.I.M.E) has been introduced in an attempt to crystallise some of the critical elements involved in determining both process and potential outcome. This may be something that individuals should note when working with and/or supporting someone who self-harms/injures to ensure that stereotyping is avoided.

References:

Allen C (1995) in Greenwood S & Bradley P (1997) Managing deliberate self-harm: the A&E perspective, *Accident and Emergency Nursing*, 5, pp134-136

BBC News (2010) Young people self-harming with sharp objects up 50%, www.bbc.co.uk/newsbeat/hi/health/newsid_8563000/8563670.stm

Barton-Breck AJT (2010) *The development of self-injury as a multi-functional behaviour*, PhD Thesis, University of Greenwich

Deacon L, Perkins C, Bellis M (2011) *Self-harm among children in the North West: accident and emergency attendance 2007-2009 and emergency hospital admissions 2007/8-2009/10*, North West Public Health Observatory, Liverpool John Moores University

Dickson S, Steeg S, Gordon M, Donaldson I, Matthews V, Kapur N, Cooper J (2011) *The Manchester Self-Harm Project: Self-Harm in Manchester January 2008 – December 2009*, University of Manchester

Lader W (2006) A Look at the Increase in Body Focused Behaviors, *Paradigm*, Winter 2006

Lewis LP, Heath NL, St Davis JM, Noble R (2011) The Scope of Non-Suicidal Self-Injury on YouTube, *Paediatrics*, Volume 127, Number 3, pp552-557

Lloyd C (1990) *Suicide and Self-Injury in Prisons: A Literature Review*, Home Office Research Study No 115, HMSO

Martin G, Swannell S, Harrison J, Hazell P, Taylor A (2010) *The Australian National Epidemiological Study of Self-Injury (ANESSI)*, Centre for Suicide Prevention Studies, Brisbane, Australia

Mind (2009) *A civilised society: mental health provision for refugees and asylum seekers in England and Wales*, www.mind.org.uk/assets/0000/5695/refugee_report_2.pdf

Mitchell KJ, Ybarra ML (2007) Online behaviour of youth who engage in self-harm provides clues for preventative intervention, *Preventative Medicine*, Volume 45, Issue 5, PP392-396

Motz A (Ed) (2009) *Managing Self-Harm: Psychological Perspectives*, Hove, Routledge

Myer T (2011) Inside Intentional Self-injury, *Nursing*, 26-31

NHS (2011) Hospital admissions for intentional self-harm increase by nearly 10,000 in three years says new report, which also shows seasonal variation in admission numbers, www.ic.nhs.uk

NIPS (2006) *Revised Self-Harm and Suicide Prevention Policy*, Northern Ireland Prison Service

Nock MK (2008) Actions speak louder than words: An elaborated theoretical model of the social functions of self-injury and other harmful behaviors, *Applied and Preventative Psychology*, 12, pp159-168

Nock(2010) Self-Injury, available at http://www.wjh.harvard.edu/~nock/nocklab/Nock_ARCP_2010.pdf

Norris ML (2007) HEADSS up: Adolescents and the Internet, *Paediatric Child Health,* Volume 12, Number 3, pp211-216

NSPCC (2009) *Young people who self-harm: Implications for public health practitioners*, Child Protection Research Briefing

O'Connor R, Rasmussen S, Miles J, Hawton K (2009) Self-harm in adolescents: self-report survey in schools in Scotland, *The British Journal of Psychiatry*, 194, pp68-72

Okahara K, Self-Injury in Japan, TIME Photos, www.time.com/photogallery/0,29307,1809157,00.html

Pembroke LR (2005) Buying into Shock, Horror and Medical Pornography, *the Cutting Edge*, Volume 15, Issue 2(58)

Richardson C (2006) *the truth about self-harm*, London, Mental Health Foundation

Webb M, Burns J, Collin P (2008) Providing online support for young people with mental health difficulties: challenges and opportunities explored, *Early Intervention in Psychiatry*, 2, pp108-113

L [age 58]

My self-harm started age 6 due to abuse by my parents and their friends.

I would hit out at walls, doors etc. And at school I deliberately fell off of gym equipment.

Doing this relieved the emotional pain inside. I was not able to tell anyone for fear of the abuse getting worse. As the years passed I started to cut my arms, wrists and even took overdoses.

I found hospital staff in the A&E departments had a hostile attitude towards not just myself but self-harm in general. I was told many times I was a wasting their time and was just looking for attention. I also had experiences of stitching with little or no anaesthetic.

At the time the medical profession I felt had very little understanding or information on self-harm.

In between visits to the A&E department I had many visits to my GP which I feel was a waste of time as he never looked into the causes of my problems. He just gave me anti depressants time after time.

It was not until the age of 38 when I had given birth to my son and daughter that the true cause of my problems emerged and social services got involved. They eventually insisted I see a therapist. I found a therapist who was survivor themselves and their understanding of self-harm was a great help to me. For the first time in years I felt I had at last found the first step to the healing process.

As the Medical Profession and I had little or no information on self-harm and there were no other support services available, I decided to start a voluntary organisation to help survivors get the support and information they needed.

Since my marriage in 1989 my family have been very understanding and supportive to me, despite all my past problems and the anguish I have put them through.

N [age 14]

First, my name is N and I am 14 years old. I started cutting end of March beginning of April of 2010.

I started for several different reasons. One reason was because my closest and dearest friend is dying in a nursing home - my mom. She was diagnosed with MS and can't even walk anymore. She is one of my biggest triggers, seeing her like that and knowing she will never be the same. Another reason is because of my dad. He emotionally and physically abuses my sisters and I, he lies about nearly everything, blames everything that has gone wrong on my mom, and deprives my siblings and I of basic needs. I hate him everyday for what he has done. He is the other major trigger I have. One of my sisters is having her own problems and doesn't live with us anymore. She has been in and out of the hospital, institutions, and now a group home.

I have also hated her for a long time. She too, self injures. Many of my family members are drug addicts and have come close to death on countless occasions. I can't lose them like that. I have nightmares of them disappearing. I have big problems in school; my oldest sister is the only one in my family to graduate high school. And I hate myself. Pretty much everything about me disgusts me. I hate my whole appearance. I am becoming anorexic, but I can't fully admit that to myself. These stories go into great detail, but that's the basics.

At first, my self-injury was just scratching my arms. My best friend at the time saw it and got really angry. As it progressed she kept yelling at me and saying that she was going to tell someone. But, she never did. A few other of my friends found out, but tried not to bring it up. I didn't think that it would get beyond the bad scratches, but it did. I started using paperclips, keys, and an arrowhead necklace. These cuts, however, were not bad enough to bleed. Still, they have left scars that I can still see perfectly fine right now. I became depressed somewhere along the way when I started middle school, and am still.

My health teacher pulled me aside before my eighth grade was over. She told me that someone said that I looked depressed. She asked me if anything was wrong. I told her about the problems stated and she felt bad for me. Then she mentioned the cuts on my arm. I thought she was going to tell my parents and I was going to get in trouble, but she promised she wouldn't. Today, sometimes I regret talking to her, or at least wish I could have changed how it went. At the beginning of summer my sister, who also SIs found out I did and told my mom. My mom started yelling at me and said it was just for attention. That really hurt, but I never talked to her about it. I stopped cutting until about halfway through the summer. It was actually the same day I found this site. I'm not blaming it, but it just triggered me. I knew I couldn't cut my arms anymore, so I cut my legs.

The first cuts weren't bad, but, one time in the bathroom was the first time I drew a fair amount of blood. I love it. I kept cutting deeper and deeper. I cut all over my thighs. Then, one day, sitting on my kitchen table was a box cutter. I didn't think I would ever actually have the nerve to use it. But I took it and hid in my room. Eventually I did use it. Small cuts at first, then deeper and worse. I started having several sessions everyday making at least four cuts each time. My trash has tons of paper towel bits drenched in blood.

At one point at the end of summer, my sister, the one who also SIs, brought it up when we were alone. She said that she knew I cut and I denied it or tried to change the subject. It was to weird and personal to talk about. She kept pushing and I tried to make it into a joke, but it didn't work. Eventually, I confessed, she didn't like that I did it but she wasn't mad at me. She only knew that I used to cut my arms. She didn't know that I now cut my legs. I left it at that for a while. Then, one night she was telling me a big secret and I told her that I had a secret, too. She really wanted to know what it was, but I was reluctant to tell her. I did in the end, but she hasn't brought it up since. I don't want her to. My other older sister knows too, she judges me, holds it against me in arguments. I don't forgive her for that.

One of my current best friends knows I cut, she used to do it, too. She always says that since she was able to stop, I can to. But I can get her to see that it isn't that easy for me. She doesn't know that it's an addiction and I can't help it, even if I wanted to. She looks at my arms almost everyday to see if there are any new cuts. I cut on my arms every now and then, but hide them with bracelets. She still sees them and still gets worried. I think she knows I cut my legs, but if she doesn't, no one does.

I've given up on trying to quit, it's too hard and I'm not strong enough. I've gone small periods of time without doing it, no more than two weeks.

I wish I was able to tell people, but I know they won't understand. They'll say that it's just for attention, they'll get mad and they'll think I'm crazy. I guess I don't want people to know. Not now, maybe not for a long time.

Cutting, depression, and suicidal thoughts have become a big part of my life. And they are here to stay for a while.

WHO SELF-HARMS / INJURES?

The aim of this section is to explore the available information in an effort to identify both those individuals and groups who appear to be more at risk of self-harm/injury. This will rely to a large extent on the current body of information that exists and is intended to include rather than be seen to exclude or marginalise this population through recognition.

What is known through some of the available material is the extent of self-harming/injuring, albeit based on those people who present seeking treatment and/or support. It is important to note this as (is perceived) the majority of people who self-harm/injure do not seek treatment and/or support.

In the US, 660,000 people were identified in a survey published in 2011. In statistics provided by The NHS Information Centre (2011) it related to accident and emergency department attendances in England and indicated that the total attendances for 'deliberate self-harm' were:

- 2008/9 – 101,670
- 2009/10 – 108,312

In the Public Health Agency Report (2009) in Northern Ireland the figure was 1,266. More detail indicated:

- Of the 1,266 episodes 54.6% were female
- Under the age of 18 years 77.4% were female
- Highest number of episodes were in the 25-34 and 35-44 age groups

In Ireland the National Registry of Deliberate Self-Harm Report (2010) indicated that there had been 11,966 presentations to hospital due to self-harm/injury and this represented a total of 9,630 individuals, overall an increase of 4% over the previous (2009) figures.

The ANESSI (2010) study in Australia suggests that if their sample population is representative of the total, then in Australia:

1.   Some 30,000 people could have sought medical help for self-harm/injury
2.   With 4,000 of this population being admitted to hospital

In the neighbouring country of New Zealand 2,465 people were hospitalised in 2008 having 'intentionally self-harmed'.

Gunnell et al (2008) in an exploration of repeat admissions of people who had been discharged from mental health care identified that 6% of them (4,935) were admitted for self-harm/injury within a twelve month period with the first month accounting for one third of the total figure.

The following brief exploration of some of the issues identified, demonstrate the variations that permeate much of the information that is available.

Klonsky et al (2003) with a focus on young people identified issues linked to increased anxiety and a heightened sensitivity to interpersonal rejection. De Leo and Heller (2005) in an Australian exploration of young people identified issues linked to exposure to self-harm in family or friends, sexual orientation worries and low self-esteem. Self-esteem is again included in the work of Laye-Gindhu and Schonert-Reichi (2005) together with emotional distress, anger problems and antisocial behaviour. Skegg (2005) reflecting a broader group than exclusively young people identifies the dual issues of socioenomic disadvantage and mental illness. Gilbert et al (2010) noted issues such as self-criticism and feelings of inferiority. Hawton and Harriss (2006) with a focus directed at older people (60+ years), identified in their work a much closer association with suicide as either an intention or increased risk in the self-harm/injury context.

It is important to highlight that certain groups of individuals are considered to be at greater risk when it comes to a range of mental health issues and self-harm/injury. Although some of the information is contentious it is important to consider. Proctor (2007) introduces the idea that if you are a woman, non-conformist and happen to self-harm/injure that there is a significant possibility of you being labelled as having a Borderline Personality Disorder. The suggestion is that self-harm/injury may be a strong determinant in the psychiatrist's thinking for arriving at this conclusion.

The groups alluded to on the previous pages are identified and discussed on these next few pages. Issues related to why some individuals may self-harm/injure will vary but it is important to note the environmental and social elements that have a significant impact on some of the individuals who are part of one or more of the following groups.

Individuals On Remand/Prisoners:

England and Wales has the highest imprisonment rate in Western Europe (SCMH, 2007) and due to the large numbers of people entering the prison system there is congestion within that system. The prison population has a disproportionately high prevalence of mental health issues and substance misuse in comparison to the general population, but the ability of the prison service to address these areas is challenging. It also has to deal with an increased suicide risk in the population, this being greatest in newly arrived prisoners within the first seven days.

Early work by Lloyd (1990) acknowledges the existence of self-harm/injury in the prison population but contains little information regarding prevalence. The Howard League for Penal Reform (2003) identified that young people were 2.2 times more likely to self-harm/injure than the adult population and that 5% of young people had self-harmed/injured in the three months of a prison service pilot project. Shaw et al (2004) identified that out of 157 self-inflicted deaths within the prison system a total of 78 (53%) had had a previous history of self-harm. Chapman and Dixon-Gordon (2010) examined emotional precursors in female prisoners who had either deliberately self-harmed or attempted suicide together with subsequent emotional consequences. They suggested a similarity in the precursor (i.e. anger) but a difference in emotional consequence; with relief related to self-harm/injury more prevalent. A study by Wright et al (2006) identified a concern of benzodiazepine use in some of the women prisoners studied together with a high prevalence of substance misuse and impulsive self-harm that together create a worrying risk factor.

The issue of people who are placed on remand or in prison is another aspect that has clearly identified a significant risk related to self-harming/injuring, particularly amongst females. The Corston Report (2007) qualifies the concern as follows:

'Self-injury is an increasing phenomenon throughout society but the levels of self-harm within some of our women's prisons and persistent self-mutilation of around 50 women in custody at any one time is shocking.'(p 12)

The Northern Ireland Prison Service (NIPS) produced revised guidance for the prison service in 2006 and indicated that:

'all staff with direct or indirect contact with prisoners must:

- Be familiar with the preventative measures that might help to prevent a prisoner harming him or herself
- be prepared to intervene and support any prisoner through a period of crisis, either individually or as a member of a multidisciplinary team
- appreciate the importance of personal contact in helping prisoners to cope with imprisonment' (p6)

Refugee/asylum seekers:

Another group that has been identified as one of concern is associated with people who are currently held in immigration detention centres. Health concerns are an issue and self-harm/injury is one aspect of this that has received increasing publicity over recent years. Freemovement is a group who provides information associated with this area. They indicate on their site that they 'provide signposting to any one in the UK subject to UK immigration controls and does not want to leave the UK, for whatever reasons' and also identify the current (2010) figures for individuals who are on 'formal self-harm at risk'. In over 11 centres the total identified figure is 1,467 people with a total of 183 incidents of self-harm requiring medical treatment.

Robjant et al (2009) carried out a systematic review of studies published in this area and identified from within this a range of health related issues, including self-harm. Mind, the mental health charity in a 2009 report, identified the challenges encountered in supporting people with mental health needs and cited information related to self-harm as one of the many issues challenging the refugee and asylum seeking population.

A recent development has been the announcement that the Commonwealth Ombudsman

(July 2011) is to investigate issues linked with this group in Australia and in particular worrying risks related to suicide and self-harm/injury.

Lesbian/gay/bisexual Individuals (LGB):

There is concern that some people who are identified as part of this group may be exposed to greater degrees of discrimination, exclusion, bullying and prejudice. All of these factors may contribute to compromise the person's mental health and create a situation where self-harm/injury becomes a greater risk. King et al (2008) carried out a systematic review of literature that explored this area and concluded that LGB people were at greater risk of self-harming/injuring than heterosexual people. Warner et al (2004) in their survey explored issues linked to rates and predictors of mental illness in this group. The results indicated that 'we found high rates of planned and actual deliberate self-harm' (p483).

Skegg et al (2003) indicated a potential correlation between increasing levels of same sex attraction and self-harm/injury. A limitation that was identified within the article stated: 'another limitation of research of this kind is that same sex attraction and self-harm will not always be disclosed, since they could be regarded as stigmatizing'. (p 545)

Youth subcultures (e.g. Goth/Emo):

Literature has emerged alongside the creation of a number of what is referred to as subcultures among young people. The two most frequently identified and explored within said literature are those mentioned here; namely Emos and Goths. Rutledge et al (2008) explore the concept of Goth culture and conclude that it attracts young people who tend to be 'depressed, feel persecuted, have a distrust of society or have suffered past abuse'. They also identify that this group/subculture have a higher prevalence of self-harm than other teen groups.

An article in the Daily Mail (Sands, 2006) entitled 'EMO cult warnings for parents' suggest that Emos see themselves as a sub-set of the Goths but the distinction 'is a celebration of self-harm'. Young et al (2007) in their published survey indicated that the Goth subculture was strongly associated with self-harm with a prevalence of 53% in the most highly identified group (n=15). They also compared this with a range of other subgroups (e.g. Punk, Heavy metal, Grunge) although it must be noted that the number related both to the Goths and others was small.

Indigenous people:

Work related to this group has been undertaken to a large extent in the Australasian context with a wealth of literature available. Hunter (2007) explores mental health in this population in rural and remote areas and although suicide is highlighted as a significant area of concern self-harm/injury is another issue that is identified. A study by Clapham et al (2006) again highlights the increased risk of self-harm in the New South Wales indigenous population but unfortunately it is related to death associated with self-harm with no alternative outcome statistics noted. A study by Mehrabadi et al (2008) looked at Aboriginal young people in two cities in Canada who were using street drugs. A range of risk issues emerged including that of self-harm/injury.

Bramley et al (2004) explored disparities across indigenous populations in Australia, New Zealand, Canada and the United States. Recognition of the vulnerability of this group in terms of high disease-specific mortality rates was observed together with a high self-harm rate among 'Canadian First Nations people'.

An alternative to this trend is seen in the work of Gater et al (2009) and Husain et al (2006) who highlight the increased risk of self-harm - particularly in women of South Asian origin - in comparison to their indigenous white counterparts.

Children/adolescents:

Although self-harm/injury is not exclusive to young people much of the readily available literature has as its focus on this very group. Smith (2008) identifies a range of possible factors that create the possibility of this group being more vulnerable. These include:

- anxiety
- eating disorders
- maltreatment
- family turmoil
- relatively late development of brain circuits

Kemp (2009) identifies that one vulnerable group who may be at greater risk by virtue of their experiences and circumstances are children and young people in care. This is also echoed in the work of Cousins et al (2008) who voice their concern regarding the vulnerability of this group and the need for a greater awareness from health care professionals. Bywaters and Rolfe (2002) indicated that those participants in their work who could identify a reason stated that experiences such as bullying, family upheaval and abuse were involved whilst memories of relief/release from a previous self-harming/injuring experience was highlighted as a reason for future repetition in a distressing or challenging situation.

A local newspaper article by Knight (2010) highlighted an increase of 80% in the number of children admitted to a local hospital after a self-harm incident. It also quoted Claire Usiskin from the YoungMinds charity as stating 'there is anecdotal evidence that the internet society and self-harming networks allow children to discuss their problems and egg each other on'.

Sourander et al (2006) in a follow-up study identified that children who had thought about or actually self-harmed/injured at the age of twelve demonstrated the potential of self-harming/injuring in later adolescence.

The Truth Hurts (2006) report indicates that young people identified a range of issues related to previous life experiences, including:

- a family member who had attempted suicide or self-harmed
- substance (drug) use in the past
- low self-image
- low self-esteem (p 22)

'Worried about self-injury?', a booklet available from YoungMinds which is a charity with a focus on children and young peoples' emotional wellbeing, highlights many of the issues already identified and in addition remembers to include such overlooked elements as:

- growing up
- pressure to fit in
- money

Some of the remaining literature that explores the various reasons, antecedents or precipitants associated with self-harming/injuring reflects the comments and information in figure 1 but also incorporates some additional outcomes, or at least different interpretations or expressions of these.

Figure 2 appeared in a report produced by Wishart (2004) as a checklist for young people to use as a means of either identifying or trying to identify their reason(s) for self-harming/injuring.

Allen (1995) cited in Greenwood & Bradley (1997), listed three reasons in broad terms; namely:

- To manage moods or feelings
- As a response to beliefs or habitual thoughts
- To communicate or manage interactions with other people

Young et al (2007) in their work indicated that the higher percentages of responses in the young people they surveyed related to:

- Relieve anger (59.5% males); (46.2% females)
- To forget about something (24.3% males); (46.2% females)
- Relieve anxiety (13.5% males); (36.5% females)

Another element that has been identified quite clearly in a recent report (Deacon et al, 2011) looking at young people presenting to accident and emergency departments in the North West of the country is that of deprivation. These children and young people were 2.3 times more likely to require emergency hospital admission. This is also mentioned, albeit briefly, in an NSPCC (2009) report looking at young people and self-harm/injury.

Older people:

The inclusion of this group of people in this section is based on the fact that they are frequently excluded in the literature related to self-harm/injury. It is also pertinent to acknowledge that although the numbers may be small that they do not merit any less attention than any other group. The ANESSI (2010) project identified that not only did a small number of older people self-harm/injure but that the onset for some had been as an older person, rather than over their adult lifespan: 'The oldest age of onset for males was 63 and for females 60'(p1).

In a recent publication by Coupland et al (2011) antidepressant use in older people was explored and some evidence emerged that suggested that some antidepressants may increase the risk of self-harm, namely SRNIs (Selective Serotonin and Norepinephrine Reuptake Inhibitors) and that this warranted further research to explore further.

Summary:

This section has explored some of the individual issues that have emerged from the literature and other sources related to the individual and potential risk issues that may be associated with self-harm/injury. It has also acknowledged that, as stated quite effectively in the 'Who Self-Injures' FirstSigns fact sheet for Parents and Guardians that:
'Self-injury affects people of all walks of life, irrespective of age, gender, sexual orientation, ethnicity or personal strength'
It is apparent that individuals within some groups would appear to have a greater risk of engaging in self-harm/injury than their peers in other groups. A variety of factors arise and some are shared across these identified groups. They include issues associated with exclusion or marginalisation, bullying and/or abuse, compromise in areas such as control. It is important to remember that irrespective of whether an individual subscribes or belongs to a particular group or belief that

is associated with an increased risk in relation to self-harm/injury, does not mean that that individual will consider or engage in self-harm/injury. It is an individual situation and not a group one!

References:

Bramley D, Hebert P, Jackson R, Chassin M (2004) Indigenous disparities in disease-specific mortality, a cross-country comparison: New Zealand, Australia, Canada, and the United States, The New Zealand Medical Journal, Volume 117, Number 1207, available at http://journal.nzma.org.nz/journal/117-1207/1215/

Bywaters P & Rolfe A (2002) *Looking beyond the scars: Understanding and responding to self-injury and self-harm*, London, NCH

Chapman AL, Dixon-Gordon KL (2010) Emotional Antecedents and Consequences of Deliberate Self-Harm and Suicide Attempts, *Suicide and Life-Threatening Behaviour*, Volume 37, Issue 5, pp543-552

Clapham KF, Stevenson MR, Kai Lo S (2006) Injury profiles of Indigenous and non-Indigenous people in New South Wales, *MJA,* 184, pp217-220

Corston J (2007) *The Corston Report*, The Home Office

Coupland C, Dhiman P, Morriss R, Arthur A, Barton G, Hippisley-Cox J (2011) Antidepressant use and risk of adverse outcomes in older people: population based cohort study, BMJ, 343:d4551 doi: 10.1136/bmj.d4551, available at http://www.bmj.com/content/343/bmj.d4551.full

Cousins W, McGowan I, Milner S (2008) Self-harm and attempted suicide in young people looked after in state care, *Journal of Children's and Young People's Nursing*, Volume 2, Number 2, pp51-54

De Loe D, Heller TS (2004) Who are the kids who self-harm? An Australian self-report survey, *MJA*, 181, pp140-144

FirstSigns (2008) LifeSigns Self-Injury Factsheet for Parents and Guardians, available at http://www.firstsigns.org.uk/publications/

Gater R, Tomenson B, Percival C, Chaudhry N, Waheed W, Dunn G, Macfarlane G, Creed F (2009) Persistent depressive disorders and social stress in people of Pakistani origin and white Europeans in UK, available at http://resources.metapress.com/pdf-preview.axd?code=124131820276w84&size=largest

Gilbert P, McEwan K, Irons C, Bhundia R, Christie R, Broomhead C, Rockliff H (2010) Self-harm in a mixed clinical population: The roles of self-criticism, shame, and social rank, British Journal of Clinical Psychology, Volume 49, Issue 4, pp563-576

Gunnell D, Hawton K, Ho D, Evans J, O'Connor S, Potokar J, Donovan J, Kapur N (2008) Hospital admissions for self-harm after discharge from psychiatric inpatient care: cohort study, BMJ, 337, a2278, available at http://www.bmj.com/content/337/bmj.a2205.full

Hawton K, Harriss L (2006) Deliberate self-harm in people aged 60 years and over: characteristics and outcomes of a 20-year cohort, International Journal of Geriatric Psychiatry, Volume 21, Issue 6, pp572-581

Hunter E (2007) Disadvantage and discontent: A review of issues relevant to the mental health of rural and remote Indigenous Australians, Australian Journal of Rural Health, 15, pp88-93

Husain MI, Waheed M, Husain N (2006) Self-harm rates in British South Asian women: psychosocial correlates and strategies for prevention, Annals of General Psychiatry, available at http://www.annals-general-psychiatry.com/content/5/1/7

Kemp R (2009) Self Harm Practice Reference Guide, National Centre for Excellence in Residential Child care (ncercc)

King M, Semlyen J, See Tai S, Killaspy H, Osborn D, Popelyuk D, Nazareth I (2008) A systematic review of mental disorder, suicide, and deliberate self-harm in lesbian, gay and bisexual people, *BMC Psychiatry*, 8:70, www.biomedcentral.com/1471-244X/8/70

Knight S (2010) *Self-harming rises by 80%*, week ending June 20th, www.kentnews.co.uk

Klonsky ED, Oltmanns TF, Turkheimer E 2003) Deliberate Self harm in a Nonclinical Population: Prevalence and Psychological Correlates, *American Journal of Psychiatry*, 160, pp1501-1508

Laye-Gindhu A, Schonert-Reichi KA (2005) Nonsuicidal Self-Harm Among Community Adolescents: Understanding the "Whats" and "Whys" of Self-Harm, *Journal of Youth and Adolescence*, Volume 34, Number 5, pp447-457

Martin G, Swannell S, Harrison J, Hazell P, Taylor A (2010) *The Australian National Epidemiological Study of Self-Injury (ANESSI)*, Centre for Suicide PreventionmStudies, Brisbane, Australia

Mehrabadi A, Paterson K, Pearce M, Patel S, Craib KJP, Moniruzzaman A, Schecter MT, Spittal PM (2008) Gender Differences in HIV and Hepatitis C Related Vulnerabilities Among Aboriginal Young People Who Use Street Drugs in Two   Canadian Cities, *Women & Health*, Volume 48, Number 3, pp235-260

Mental Health Foundation (2006) *Truth Hurts: Report of the National Inquiry into Self-harm among Young People*

Ministry of Health (2010) Suicide Facts: *Deaths and Intentional self-harm hospitalisations* 2008, Wellington, Ministry of Health

National Hospital Ambulatory Medical Care Survey: 2008 Emergency Department Summary Tables, available at http://www.cdc.gov/nchs/data/ahcd/nhamcs_emergency/nhamcsed2008.pdf

National Suicide Research Foundation (2011) *National Registry of Deliberate Self Harm Annual Report 2010*, Cork, National Suicide Research Foundation

NHS Information Centre (2011) *Accident and Emergency Attendances in England (Experimental Statistics), 2009-10*

NIPS (2006) *Revised Self-Harm and Suicide Prevention Policy*, Northern Ireland Prison Service

Proctor G (2007). Disordered Boundaries? A Critique of 'Borderline Personality Disorder' in Spandler H, Warner S (Eds), *Beyond Fear And Control: working with young people who self-harm*, Herefordshire, PCCS Books, Chapter 7

Public Health Agency (2009) *Northern Ireland Registry of DSH: Western Area Annual Report 2009,* available at http://www.dhsspsni.gov.uk/self-harm_registry_2009_annual_report.pdf

Robjant K, Hassan R, Katona C (2009) Mental health implications of detaining asylum seekers: systematic review, *The British Journal of Psychiatry,* 194, pp306-312

Rutledge CM, Rimer D, Scott M (2008) Vulnerable Goth Teens: The Role of Schools in This Psychosocial High Risk Culture, *Journal of School Health*, Volume 78, Issue 9, pp459-464

Sands S (2006) EMO cult culture warning for parents, Daily Mail

SCMH (2007) *Mental health care in prisons*, Briefing 32

Shaw J, Baker D, Hunt IM, Moloney A, Appleby L (2004) Suicide by prisoners, *British Journal of Psychiatry*, 184, pp263-267

Skegg K, Nada-Raja S, Dickson N, Paul C, Williams S (2003) Sexual Orientation and Self-Harm in Men and Women, *American Journal of Psychiatry,* 160, pp541-546

Skegg K (2005) Self-Harm, *The Lancet*, Volume 366, Issue 9495, pp1471-1483

Smith BD (2008) Adolescent Nonsuicidal Self-Injury: Evaluation and Treatment, *Psychiatric Times*, Volume 25, Number 7

Sourander A, Aromaa M, Pihlakoski L, Haavisto A, Rautava P, Helenius H, Sillanpaa M (2006) Early predictors of deliberate self-harm among adolescents. A prospective follow-up study from age 3 to age 15, *Journal of Affective Disorders*, Volume 93, Issue 1, pp87-96

The Howard League for Penal Reform (2003) *Busy doing nothing: Young men on remand*, London

Warner J, McKeown E, Griffin M, Johnson K, Ramsay A, Cort C, King M (2004) Rates and predictors of mental illness in gay men, lesbians and bisexual men and women: Results from a survey based in England and Wales, *The British Journal of Psychiatry*, 185, pp479-485

Wishart M (2004) *Adolescent Self-Harm: An Exploration of the Nature and prevalence in Banyule/Nillumbik*, Nillumbik Community Health Service, p 38

Wright B, Duffy D, Curtin K, Linehan S, Monks S, Kennedy HG (2006) Psychiatric morbidity among women prisoners newly committed and amongst remanded and sentenced women in the Irish prison system, *Irish Journal of Psychiatric Medicine*, Volume 32, Number 2, pp47-53

Young R, Van Beinum M, Sweeting H, West P (2007) Young people who self-harm, *The British Journal of Psychiatry*, 191, pp 44-49

E [age 19]

Self harm. Self-mutilation. Cutting. Self-injury. Type any of them into Google and you get about 3,080,000 results. NICE guidelines will tell you that it's, "self-poisoning, or injury, irrespective of the apparent purpose of the act." But none of these give a good picture of what self-harm is to me.

I am E. Lots of things make me who I am. I'm 19, I am a student, I work part time in a shop and I'm always keeping busy. Self-harm does not change who I am despite it being a part of my life for 6 years now. For me self-harm is a way of coping. By cutting myself I can calm down, think clearly and see things from a different perspective. Self-harm is my way of staying alive.

Just before I first self harmed I was struggling and no-one wanted to listen or take me seriously. I was seen by the CAMHs team yet they didn't seem to care and   discharged me. And why shouldn't they? To them I was no different to the next stroppy teenager. But something made me different; something made me make that first cut. And I still don't know why, I just know that straight after when I saw the blood I realised how much of an idiot I had been.

I promised myself never to do it again and never to tell anyone. Again, I'm not sure what happened but things got bad again a couple of days later. I knew from magazines that other people self harmed and realised that they would only do it if it helped them and I decided to cut myself again. It made me feel totally different. I was powerful and in control, and everything in my head just fell into place and everything that was bad didn't matter anymore.

As far I as I was concerned I was fine, so OK my arms were a mess but this amazing thing was helping me through life, it made everything feel OK. Of course no-one else took my view, and I started attending

CHAMs every week. I hated the nurse. She made me show her my cuts, tell her what tool I had used and tried to dress them. All things that I can't stand doing or talking about. Self-harm is something that had already become very private. It made me feel stronger that I could do it and hide it and dressing it would mean that I cared for myself; that would make me weak. I wish that I had the opportunity to have talked more about how I was feeling and tried to stop all the thoughts in my head. Maybe that would have stopped the chain of events that had followed.

My parents were told about my self-harm by the nurse. They just cried, then searched my room and watched me all the time to try and stop me self-harming. For a time I did try to stop but realised that it just wasn't worth it, because stopping only made everything worse. Distractions just meant I bottled everything up and when I did give in and self-harm, I would cut more and deeper than before. I never spoke to my parents about it and never will. Being forced to talk to them just made me hide it more. I wanted to protect them from the truth that their child was hurting. Because this hurt was too much for her to handle and there was nothing they could have done to take it away.

I carried on through life for the next year, some days good, others bad. I was determined that no-one should know. My parents seemed to forget about it and although I carried on seeing a mental health nurse I had even convinced her I was fine. But just to be sure before discharging me I was sent me to art therapy.
I wish they just left me alone, because about 3 months later I cracked. I wanted to die. I was sent back to therapy and self-harm became my new best friend. Any thoughts I had about wanting to stop had gone. I needed it; I needed something that would always be there for me. Something to keep me alive.

Again another year passed and I was admitted as an inpatient. They were some of the worst months of my life. I was fighting my head every day; too scared to let anyone help me. But it was the first time that I had ever met others who self harmed. I found it hard to deal with them hurting themselves and being so open about it. I was very discrete when I self harmed and no-one knew about it. Which was definitely for the best; I didn't want to be dragged down by all the other girls who cut themselves together. I find those six months the hardest to think about. The hospital didn't help me, they couldn't. They didn't listen.

On being discharged the hospital I pretended that everything was fine, only for me to be sent back to my therapist her believing I was fixed. They hadn't scratched the surface. I had to learn to trust her again. I needed to talk about being an inpatient and learn to deal with the fact I was alive. The fact that I hadn't been listened to in the hospital, just made it harder for me to talk.

Since then I have moved onto adult services and I finally feel like I am being listened to. But it's taking time for me to trust them. Self-harm is still a big part of my life and right now I don't want to stop. I need it to get through every day.

On the surface I am "normal"; I present this mask to the world because I need to keep everything inside me. I don't want to upset anyone but I feel like I have failed because I self harm. Many people think it's a stroppy teenager thing and maybe it is for some people, maybe it was for me. But now it's real and something that I need to keep me alive. I hate hiding who I am from people, I have never been able to tell anyone I self harm. Anyone who knows - knows by accident. I keep people at arm's length; I can't deal with my life right now and I can't expect anyone else to.

Self-harm has definitely changed who I am, and I hate the person it's made me. But it's something that has always been there for me. Even when I haven't

understood what has been wrong, somehow it's always
made me feel better.

H [age 36]

I am H, a 36 year old female and a part time student living in Kent. I have been self-injuring since I was 30, triggered by a rape occurring abroad where I was living and teaching. This bought back traumatic childhood memories of physical and sexual abuse by my father. I started injuring myself to just get through the day, either in the morning to enable me to get to work or in the evening when I got home to cope with the exhaustion of the day. I hid the marks by wearing long sleeves even when it was very hot and when a friend saw I just said they were cat scratches.

It became harder and harder to get through the day but I was determined not to self-injure at work, I was not coping though and eventually asked a friend and colleague for help and started seeing a psychiatrist and taking anti-depressants, although eventually I had to give up my job and come back to the UK. I tried to make a fresh start and go back to work part time but soon the stress became too much again. I began self-injuring to get through the day, once again I asked for help and was referred to my GP and then onto the local mental health team and was allocated a Social Worker. My self-injury continued becoming an increasing risk to my health and I had three short-term stays in a psychiatric unit.

I was diagnosed with a different mental illness depending on which doctor I saw but I still believe I was just suffering from post-traumatic stress symptoms and am not Bipolar or suffering from Borderline Personality Disorder. I have had long term counselling to work through everything and am finally coming to terms with past events and the thought of a future life becoming less scary.

The effect of self-injuring has changed over time for me, the initial release reduced stressful feelings, but as my emotions seemed to become more intense the physical pain became a way to mask the emotional pain. Feelings of guilt, shame, self-hatred, anger, despair and hopelessness seemed to dominate the day and the night. Flashbacks and nightmares increased as more memories returned. Eventually I started to experience a form of dissociation when feelings became too traumatic and self-injury was the only way I could bring myself back to the present. I often did not remember the actual act of self-injury but the need to deal with the consequences and get to the hospital for treatment would be a practical thing to focus on and the pain came later. My self-injuring became the only thing that made me feel alive, as if I needed to see my life force externally.

The reaction of people when finding out that I self-injure has varied enormously. I first told a close friend on the phone when I was still abroad, she refused to speak to me after that and is still of the opinion that I need to "pull my socks up and sort myself out" I don't see her much now. The first person in my family that I told was my sister, I don't think she really understood but she did try and brought me some books on depression when she came to visit and I have now talked to her about everything and we are becoming close. My mum however, was of the unhelpful opinion that I needed to "grow up and stop being stupid". I still have some close friends from 'before' who have accepted me as I am and supported me through everything, but others have kept their distance. I have new friends now that I have met through the church that I began to attend, they are now my family and have got me through to the point where I now have not self-injured for ten months and it is down to their understanding and unfailing support.

Becoming a Christian was a life changing decision and I believe I have a real Father now who loves me, will not hurt me and who I can always trust. I am now not ashamed and am quite open about self-harm and I wear short sleeves when it is hot in most situations, I will always answer questions about my scars honestly now and try to educate peoples ignorance as much as possible. There are so many myths still existing and hence people suffering in silent secrecy.

I wanted to stop for a long time but just couldn't, there seemed no other way to survive and that was exactly what it was – survival, staying alive. The words 'support mechanism' just don't seem to cover it. Gradually I started trying new ways to cope, it was a long slow process but I was self-injuring less and less. The situation was still life threatening and I knew I had to decide to live and started phoning friends before injuring, going the minor injuries unit to stay safe instead of to get treatment.

The understanding and non-judgemental attitude of all but one of the Nurse Practitioners was a real key to being able to feel safe to go there. Learning to recognise the early signs of emotional distress and talk to someone who genuinely cared about me was the way I started to, and am still coping. I am still having counselling and still struggle on a daily basis but I have learnt that my friends really do love me and that maybe that means I can love myself. If friends are not available at that critical moment I no longer feel abandoned by them but know that I can talk to God who is always there for me and that helps me not to feel alone. I still need a friend and a hug as soon as I can find one though.

I am not going to say I will never self-injure again, it is an addiction that I could easily return too and will remain a daily struggle. Although I have had and still have a lot of help and support from health professionals, the real help and hope has been from friends and their love. Better than any medication available anywhere.

SELF-HARM/INJURY AND SUICIDE?

Having already explored the rationale for the title of this particular book, we can now turn our attention to the sensitivities linked to the area of self-harm/injury and its implied or actual link to/with suicide. This may be characterised by the interaction between the person who self-harm/injures and practitioners they encounter who are invariably informed that they need to assess the individual to be able to distinguish whether the individual has attempted suicide or has self-harmed/injured. This is an area that can therefore create conflict between individuals and services (e.g. in the accident and emergency department of the hospital) due to what the person may feel is an inappropriate inference.

If/when an individual presents to a service such as health seeking help and support after an episode of self-harm/injury they will be involved in interventions to address their physical/medical needs and to assess the intent related to the harm/injury that has occurred. This has not always been the case and only became clear with the guidance issued by NICE (2004) in the early part of this century. Before this it was customary for anyone who presented to health practitioners having harmed/injured themselves to be assessed only if the practitioner believed it was a suicide attempt (e.g. overdose).

If the person was deemed to have self-harmed/injured (frequently noted through physical injuries) and not considered to have been attempting to end their life they would often have their physical injury attended to and then be discharged. There was often little or no attempt to explore with the person how the injury had taken place and seldom any offer of the opportunity to talk and be assessed if that was seen to be of assistance. Although this has improved considerably in terms of how people are now received, it has led to people who present with self-harm/injury being frequently treated in a similar fashion to those who have attempted suicide. This can be difficult if the person has taken an overdose as this has historically been linked to suicide or attempted suicide. The literature does not necessarily assist in distinguishing the difference and this may on occasion be deemed an oversight rather than a deliberate attempt to continually relate the two concepts (self-harm/injury and suicide). This is demonstrated quite well in an early work by Lloyd (1990) looking at suicide and self-harm in prisons where he indicates: 'It could be, therefore, that cases of self-injury which closely resemble suicide represent genuine 'suicide attempts''(p25). Again in an article by McElroy and Sheppard (1999) in the summary on the first page it is stated that: 'Individuals with problems of self-poisoning and self-injury have placed increasing pressure on general hospital staff involved in their care. There should therefore be adequate services for suicide attempters in every general hospital.'(p 66) This may be an oversight in an article that is exploring the assessment and management of self-harming patients.

King et al (2008) report in their systematic review of literature that in looking at mental disorder, suicide and deliberate self-harm in lesbian, gay and bisexual people that the distinction between suicide and self-harm/injury was often unclear. The World Health Organisation (WHO, 2009) in a report looking at women and reproductive mental health discuss self-harm but principally in the context of suicide and death with little in the way of self-harm as a life preserving strategy.

Martin et al (2010) in an exploration of self-injury in Australia identified a number of issues in their survey including:

- Age ranges of between lower 10-14 band to 75-84 upper band

- Adults who self-injured were more likely to have received a psychiatric diagnosis
- Self-injurers were at higher risk of suicidal thoughts and behaviour

A Community Affairs References Committee Report (2010) referred to suicide in Australia and indicated in the data related to indigenous communities that: 'Of the 2,472 deaths registered across Australia in 2008 where the deceased person was identified as being of Aboriginal or Torres Strait origin, 103 were coded as Intentional self-harm [suicide]'. Another Australian source from SANE (2010) explores the relationship between mental illness, suicide and self-harm and indicated that its questionnaire sample of people (n=285) indicated that 'Almost half of those who self-harmed (45%) wanted to end their life at that time.'

In the way of redressing this 'link' is a statement by Pritchard (1996) in his book where he states: 'Perhaps the most difficult practice problem is coming to terms with the fact that while suicide is associated with deliberate self-harm, DSH is not always, thankfully, associated with eventual suicide.' (p 77)

Strong (1998) in her excellent book entitled 'A Bright Red Scream' reflects a similar clarity in the differentiation when stating: 'While most self-injurers are suicidal from time to time, and may even become suicidal over their inability to stop cutting, the two behaviours serve very different ends.'(p 32) Holmes (2010) in a booklet that explores youth self-harm and suicide indicates that the reasons related to self-harm/injury are many but: 'it would be wrong to assume that everybody who engages in self-harm is suicidal, and equally it would be incorrect to assume that everybody who engages in self-harm is depressed' (p5)

If, as mentioned in the previous chapter we consider the idea of a spectrum of self-harm it has been suggested that this model could encompass suicide as part of that total spectrum as demonstrated in figure five on the following page. This looks at self-harm purely in terms of the amount of harm that is inflicted and the required intervention(s) rather than additional elements such as motivation and intent.

Opponents of this approach may argue that all of the requisite elements need to be taken into consideration. If these were taken into consideration then a different model would emerge as indicated in figure six. This approach identifies that the intent, belief and action focus are distinctive. In rare situations death can be a consequence in both suicide and self-harm/injury if the outcome is so extreme or life threatening that the individual does not survive.

Figure 5: The Self-Harm Spectrum

Extreme	Severe	Serious	Moderate	Mild
Resulting in death, intended or not	Resulting in significant injury or risk of death, requiring urgent intervention and/or *medical attention	Resulting in injury or outcome that requires *medical attention	Resulting in injury that may require intervention by the individual or others, including *medical	Resulting in injury that does not require medical attention

*medical – in this context medical refers to a Doctor or nurse linked to general health rather than mental health.

Sorensen (2009) in his attempt to explore what initially was a question related to suicide presents a model that he refers to as the 'suicide ladder'. This is replicated in PDF format from his initial response posted in 2009. He suggests that generally, deliberate self-harm does not link or relate to suicide but in some individuals it might constitute a rehearsal for what he refers to as 'the final act'. The difference between this and figure five above would appear to exist in the belief that self-harm/injury may be used as a form of rehearsal for later suicide as opposed to self-harm being considered something that people engage in which may have an undetermined outcome.

Risk assessment literature will often consider the need to explore what the individual intended as part of the process of distinguishing life ending (suicide) as a potential outcome compared to life maintaining (self-harm/injury). Importantly some organisations look at death as not necessarily being the objective for someone in extreme distress where the concept of suicide is being explored. In discussion with colleagues from one organisation who have had considerable experience in talking to people in very distressed states, there emerged a belief that the person may just wish to escape from their current situation. The desperation or immediacy of this need resulted in a focus based on 'escape' without necessarily being fully aware of the consequence. The awareness of death as a permanent and finite outcome was not necessarily something the individual had consciously incorporated into their 'plan'. This is an important point for consideration when talking to people in extreme distress but is not within the remit of the self-harm/injury focus that this work addresses.

The third model (figure seven) accommodates the approach that self-harm is a broad term encapsulating a range of behaviour. Within it is a more specific behaviour that is distinctive enough to separate out, namely self-injury. The difficulty perceived with this model is the exact understanding of what self-injury actually constitutes. If it is based on an external process like cutting or burning for example then the appearance of SI would be markedly less within the figure. If however we look at self-injury as a medical or clinical process then there is a much greater similarity between the concept of self-harm and self-injury.

Much of the debate centres around the clinical inclusion/exclusion criteria frequently associated with the DSM-IV and ICD-10 classifications as mentioned previously. Some organisations/groups (e.g. FirstSigns, Anxiety Zone) are quite clear in their distinction that self-harm is broader than the diagnostic classifications, whilst many others use terms such as self-harm and self-injury interchangeably.

Figure 6: Suicide v Self-Harm

	Intent	Belief	Action focus	Consequence
Self-harm	To live	Will help (even if short-term)	**Harm, Injury**	Relief, pain, guilt, hope
Suicide	To 'escape' from significant issue, distress.	Will or hope to 'escape'	**Escape** from 'issue', (intended) results in death (not necessarily intended)	Death

A range of literature exists that appears to do little to reduce the confusion by discussing self-harm/injury and suicide, almost as if they were as one. The work of Young et al (2007) and O'Connor et al (2009) mentioned previously identified that young people in their survey when questioned about reasons why they had self-harmed/injured included responses that identified some uncomfortable issues. Reasons given included both those generally associated with self-harming/injuring (e.g. to gain relief, to forget) but also quite highly placed on the lists of both pieces of work were expressions more closely associated with the area of suicide (e.g. the wish to die, to kill myself) as an expressed intention.

Figure 7: Self-Harm (SH) v Self-injury (SI)

ACTIVITY	MEDICAL/CLINICAL CONCEPT	EXTERNAL/INTERNAL CONCEPT
Overdose of drugs	SH/SI	SH
Burning (external)	SI	SI
Swallowing substances	SH/SI	SH
Cutting	SI	SI
Scalding	SI	SI
Inhaling substances	SH/SI	SH
Alcohol abuse	SH	SH
Drug abuse	SH	SH
Eating disorders	SH	SH

Vollm and Dolan (2009) indicated that in their screening of women prisoners almost 46% had either self-harmed or attempted suicide. Specifically 8.6% had self-harmed with no suicide intent while 16.5% had attempted suicide with no intention to self-harm/injure. This element separates the two concepts quite clearly but also highlights the challenges faced by both women in prison and those charged with a responsibility to support them.

It is important to acknowledge that there are within the exploration of the two concepts a number of obvious relationships apparent. Some of the issues that can be seen to be shared and need to be carefully assessed to determine distinctions include the following:

- Risk – both suicide and self-harm/injury include an element of risk to the safety of the individual irrespective of the motivation behind the activity
- Method – there is an overlap here in terms of various methods employed by the individual, most notably overdose.
- Outcome –here the 'planned' outcome considered by the person may be different from the actual outcome. For example the person who intended to live may die due to the severity and nature of the self-harm/injury
- Intervention – irrespective of the intention all individuals who are seen by practitioners should now be offered assessment. This includes both self-harm/injury and attempted suicide.
- 'Post' harm/injury risk – there is statistically a recognisable increased risk related to people who self-harm/injure regarding future suicide

Despite the above points and particularly the final one it is worth noting that this equally applies to a range of other areas as well; i.e. mental illness [e.g. depression], recent discharge from a mental health unit [e.g. service users]. Just because risks are statistically greater in relation to suicide does not mean that the person will! This is something that appears to get overlooked and requires a balanced approach to be taken. An example offered to highlight this perceived relationship comes from the Reach Out National Strategy for Action on Suicide   Prevention (Ireland) published in 2005 in its definition of key terms:

'Deliberate Self-Harm – The various methods by which people deliberately harm themselves, including self-cutting and taking overdoses. Varying degrees of suicide intent can be present and sometimes there may not be any suicidal intent, although an increased risk of further suicidal behaviour is associated with all DSH'. (p9)

Another document by Cadman and Hoy (2009) in their exploration of the working definitions section highlights the importance of distinguishing: 'between self-harm that is motivated by the intention to end one's life and self-harm that is without suicidal intent' (p29). This is discussed in the context of clinicians having access to a wide range of rather general definitions that do not necessarily assist in the process of attempting to distinguish individual's actual intent.

Bywaters and Rolfe (2002) in their exploration of 'what is self-injury?' section continue the theme that is all too familiar by highlighting the various terms in use, including interpretations by professionals and those who self-harm/injure and the general confusion that permeated much of the available literature. They indicated that their focus would be on 'deliberately self-damaging behaviour which is not intended to be life threatening' (p1) and that their use of self-injury was not meant to exclude other aspects of behaviour where people caused harm but 'simply to avoid always having to write 'self-injury and self-harm''.

My own interpretation evolved over a period of time starting from when I first became specifically interested listening to a variety of health and social care practitioners and other people, including service users, together with extensive reading around the subject area. This led me to consider that harm as the central activity remained constant but other issues (e.g. intent, emotional status, process, and outcome) might vary. This led to the following definition emerging for self-harm:

'The inflicting of harm to a greater or lesser extent, either in an attempt to deal with psychological distress or to escape from the existing state of being, with or without the intention to end life'.(Wallace, 2012)

It is difficult to determine whether I have dramatically changed this view although I concede that many individuals hold a strong belief that no relationship exists between a process that may have a stated intent to save life and one that may focus on an end to life. Where an explicit statement has been expressed by an individual in terms of initial intention this would appear to introduce clarity into the process. Unfortunately this has on occasion been compromised by some individuals who, although apparently limited in number, have indicated that the process of attempting to deal with their distress may start with an agenda (e.g. to preserve life) and at some point this agenda may alter (e.g. end life) or vice versa.

This adds further to the state of uncertainty because it indicates that although we may decide on a course of action for a number of varying reasons that the course of action itself may alter as consideration of the issues and potential resolutions does not necessarily remain constant during the actual event of dealing with the distress.

Despite this ambivalence, it is important that practitioners try to distinguish the individual's intention when they actually engaged in the harm/injury. This requires a sensitive exploration with the individual and their recollection of whether they were trying to end their life or not, particularly in situations such as for example an overdose. It is also important to remember to retain a focus on the person rather than the event during this process. Here it is important that the practitioner clearly explains what they are doing and saying and why, to help the individual understand why they are being asked these particular questions. A failure to do this can result in the individual feeling that they are being inappropriately dealt with and may make them feel more distressed.

Although much of this discussion revolves around the difficulty that many practitioners face when attempting to differentiate between what might have been a suicide attempt or self-harm/injury, there is a need to recognise that within this area the boundaries are often blurred. The continuing debate and exploration of both differences and similarities may eventually result in something that offers a more distinct clarification than currently exists. The multitude of terms in use, together with the various differing interpretations does little to aid this process at present. There is a role for all parties in this process and that includes all; i.e. practitioners, groups/organisations, researchers, service users. I have not included those individuals who do not access, use or notify services, as currently these individuals are principally known only to themselves and therefore unlikely to influence the debate unless they choose to become actively involved. This will require both courage and a change of attitude that leads to a reduction in the potential that exists in people attempting to interpret motivation (e.g. attention-seeking!) in people who as FirstSigns label it, are 'coming out'.

Although practitioners such as doctors and nurses have progressed in their knowledge regarding self-harm/injury, due to an increase in the number of courses, programmes and workshops available there is unfortunately still a degree of misunderstanding that exists. This occasionally translates into poor practice on the part of the practitioner resulting in the individual who has arrived for help and support potentially feeling worse than they did when they made the decision to attend. This is counterproductive as bad experiences often translate into a reduction in motivation to attend in future should the need arise and to possibly share that experience with others who may also then decide likewise.

In summary although it can be very difficult for practitioners to distinguish on some occasions whether the individual wanted to, put in its simplest form, live or die through the activity they engaged in, it is important that practitioners approach the issue sensitively. This includes, most importantly, the ability to communicate what is taking place during the interaction with the service user and the reasons behind it.

It is now recognised more than ever before that the service user is the expert and needs to be listened to. The process of engagement and assessment should be one of collaboration and must take into account many of the points already raised including respect, acknowledgement, acceptance, sensitivity and privacy. It should also continue to acknowledge the need for consent from the service user as an integral part of the process.

Summary:

It is apparent within the main body of published literature that some link exists between people who self-harm/injure and those who attempt or complete suicide. Whether this is direct or indirect is of little value in terms of the debate at this point but the fact remains that there is sufficient statistical evidence to indicate that for some people who self-harm/injure there is a raised risk of them at some point in their lives attempting or completing suicide. It is important to note that we are considering a percentage of the population who self-harms/injures and that percentage is not constant, even within the literature available. It is also important to note that circumstances in peoples' lives are constantly in a process of change so even if some individuals are noted to have self-harmed/injured and subsequently attempted or completed suicide that the issues may have been totally different and the actions separate. This may avoid the temptation to try to 'force' a link between what may in fact be totally unconnected actions other than through the fact that they were linked via that one person.

References:

Bywaters P & Rolfe A (2002) *Looking beyond the scars: Understanding and responding to self-injury and self-harm*, London, NCH

Cadman L & Hoy J (2009) *Cutting the Risk: Self-Harm Minimisation in Perspective – Teaching and learning Guidelines*, Mind, p29

Health Services Executive, The National Suicide Review Group and Department of Health and Children (2005) *Reach Out: National Strategy for Action on Suicide prevention 2005-2014*, p9

Holmes K (2010) *Youth Self-Harm and Suicide*, YSPI Services Limited

King M, Semlyen J, See Tai S, Killaspy H, Osborn D, Popelyuk D, Nazareth I (2008) A systematic review of mental disorder, suicide, and deliberate self-harm in lesbian, gay and bisexual people, *BMC Psychiatry*, Volume 8:70, www.biomedcentral.com/1471-244X/8/70

Lloyd C (1990) *Suicide and Self-Injury in Prison: A Literature Review*, Home Office Research Study No 115, HMSO

Martin G, Swannell SV, Hazell PL, Harrison JE, Taylor AW (2010) Self-injury in Australia: a community survey, MJA, Volume 193, Number 9, pp506-510

McElroy A, Sheppard G (1999) The assessment and management of self-harming patients in an Accident and Emergency department: an action research project, *Journal of Clinical Nursing*, 8, pp66-72

O'Connor R, Rasmussen S, Miles J, Hawton K (2009) Self-harm in adolescents: self-report survey in schools in Scotland, *The British Journal of Psychiatry*, 194, pp68-72

Pritchard C (1996) Suicide *–The Ultimate Rejection? A psycho-social study*, Buckingham, OU Press

SANE (2010) Suicide, self-harm and mental illness, Research Bulletin 11, available at http://www.sane.org/images/stories/information/research/rb11.pdf

Senate Community Affairs Committee Secretariat (2010) The Senate – Community Affairs References Committee - *The Hidden Toll: Suicide in Australia*

Sorensen,S (2009) A question about suicide assessment, http://stuartsorensen.files.wordpress.com/2010/08/sps-suicide-assessment-summary.pdf

Strong M (1998) *A Bright Red Scream*, Middlesex, Penguin Books

Vollm BA, Dolan MC (2009) Self-harm among UK female prisoners: a cross-sectional study, *The Journal of Forensic Psychiatry & Psychology*, Volume 20, Number 5, 741-751

Wallace,B (2012) *Self-Harm/Injury: An Exploration of attitudes and issues from literature and personal stories*, Brentwood, Chipmunkapublishing

WHO (2009) *Mental health aspects of women's reproductive health: A global review of the literature*, World Health Organisation

Young R, Van Beinum M, Sweeting H, West P (2007) Young people who self-harm, *The British Journal of Psychiatry*, 191, pp44-49

O [age 15]

I'm 15 now, but the first time I ever heard of self-harm was when a girl in my class mentioned the word 'emo' when I was in year 5. She said that they slit their wrists with their locker keys, which confused us all, and we asked why but she said she didn't know.

The first time I ever saw real evidence was in year 6, when they boy who sat next to me came into school with a large cut on his arm, which he said he'd done.

I was really confused, so I asked him why, he said it just makes you feel better.

By the time I'd entered year 9, I knew what self-harm was and thought I was the last person who'd ever do it. Then a girl in my class, who I wasn't very close to but knew well enough, began self-harming. I was confused but my first reaction was to just accept it and accept that there was nothing I could do.

I ended year 9 with a boyfriend, who in the summer forced me to do things that I didn't want to do, in the end constituting rape. I buried it for a long time, as a result having severe depression and post-traumatic stress disorder, which lasted for quite a while. At the same time, I was also trying to support; two friends who self-harmed, one with bulimia, a friend with a severe split personality disorder and another friend whose father had just died suddenly.

I went to see my GP and they referred me to counselling, although my parents just thought it was me being hormonal. They insisted if I ever started self-harming I should call them.

It was a struggle to cope with supporting all my friends, as well as increasing schoolwork and the confusion and depression I was experiencing. After what had happened in the summer and in November, mid December and new-year I seriously contemplated suicide. When it snowed I gathered snow from my window into my hands, held it for a while then ran my hands under hot water, which felt like extreme burning, but it just wasn't enough.

It was around New Year that the feelings of loneliness and uselessness became too much, and with a set of mini screwdrivers were in my hand and I undid the sharpener blade on my pencil sharpener. It was totally impulsive, and odd, as I had always been afraid of pain before, but I cut the top of my forearm about 6 times. Not too deep. The weird thing was that afterwards I felt so much better, like I'd let all the bottled up feelings out, and got an amazing high. It then became normal for me to cut both arms, sometimes up to three times a day and twenty cuts each time. Both my arms were completely covered in cuts, and I took to wearing a long sleeved top in PE just to hide it. But each time I did it, all my problems felt like they were gone. Somewhere, I knew it was wrong, but my argument for carrying on was that I needed to support my friends, and if I was an emotional mess I couldn't do it – cutting for me sorted out my mess. If I carried on, I could help my friends to be ok. I never called the GP. The only time I felt regret was when I felt the stinging sensation under my sleeves.

At the end of January, I was on work experience when I had a large nosebleed after tripping over in the office. After some persuasion, I was taken to see the company nurse who wanted to take my blood pressure. I protested, I didn't need it, but she insisted. She didn't say anything about my arm. I thought I had got away with it. Then she asked if anyone else knew. I said yes and walked out of the room but I couldn't stop remembering how sad and pitying her expression had been and I made up my mind to stop. I spoke with my friends who self-harmed and we agreed to stop together.

It was unbelievably hard, and I failed within a week. My friends then learnt about it, and it was sometimes hard because I'd see their wrists and feel jealous. I still wore long sleeves, and I told my parents, which was unbelievably hard, my mum started crying which was even harder because a few months back she said if she had a child that self-harmed she would feel that she had failed as a parent.

My best friend found out, and she was extremely upset, which made me feel even worse and I decided to try as hard as possible to stop.

I managed to get cutting down to once a week, or few weeks if I was lucky. It was end of February when I threw my sharpener blade out of the window.

I felt so powerful, with that throw, it took a while to get the guts to do it, but I did it. I was tempted for a while to go and get it again, but I didn't.

In the next few weeks, my friend's split personality problem became worse, and he would really upset me without understanding, as he has no concept of empathy. At these times I would have panic attacks, and the only way to calm down was to cut, so I unscrewed another blade on a sharpener, which was sharper. I cut just below my elbow, my knee, thigh and ankle. Another regular place became my hips and waist, as they were covered by clothes all the time and healed quickly with minimal scarring.

My arms were a total mess and my mum got me bio-oil, which helped them to fade. Altogether I had well over 300 scars on my arms, and a few on my hands. I felt the desire to cut all the time, really strongly, to the point where I had to ask to go to the toilet in the middle of lessons and run my hands under cold water, which seemed to calm me down, and just talk myself through what would happen if I started cutting again.

Around mid March, I was taken out of a school activity in hysterics because I had been put accidentally in a group with my ex-boyfriend and it was just too much for me. I was taken to a really kind teacher who spoke it all through with me and we made the decision to talk to the police about it, which is one of the hardest decisions of my life. Although I knew it was the right one, it was absolutely terrifying.

When I did talk to the police, it was extremely hard and I couldn't say any of it, so they had to ask me to write it down. Afterwards I felt better, and I made decisions, although I didn't pursue any cases against him. At the end of the week though, I felt extremely guilty and cut my waist to stop the feelings. This was I think the last time it happened.

Some people have seen them at school but not too many comment, they just look a bit scared, which I feel guilty about sometimes. The scars on my arms change colour in different temperatures, so sometimes you can't see them, and sometimes they are really vivid. A few people in my class know and they are quite supportive, I've also found out about a lot of other people who used to cut, that I never knew about.

I'm still supporting my other friends who self-harm and its easier now to understand why they did, and although we all tried to stop together, we now understand that the desire to cut doesn't really disappear, it just lies dormant.

Last week our form had injections, and I had to rub my arms to warm them so the scars would fade, but I think people are quite blind, and don't usually notice things unless you mention something, so that makes me feel better. I hate it when people think that it is an attention-seeking thing, or for people who are stupid and just can't cope. I really hate it when people laugh about it and think self-harm is just a joke. I also hate how it's not covered in PSHE, because I think if people had known about it, and it wasn't such a shameful thing, and teachers were trained to know what to do instead of giving people detentions over it, a lot of those who do self-harm wouldn't have.

It may have been a stupid decision but I honestly think in the short term it helped to save my life. Maybe I'm crazy but I'm still here.

I'm still waiting for the counselling, but I haven't cut in over a month and a half. The desire to do it is still there sometimes, but it's a rare occurrence now. I keep my blade in my purse, but that's mainly for reassurance as I don't use it anymore, and the other ones I had are now lost. Sometimes I feel proud of my scars, as they're proof that I have lived and I have a story, but a lot of the time I'm ashamed of them and try to hide them.

I hope one day my mind won't even think about doing it.

Thank you

R [age 30's]

I don't know why I self-harmed. I don't know what actually happened in my head to make me start and I don't know what then occurred to make me stop. I don't know what maintained the harming for so long and I don't know what stops me going back but it's okay not to understand self-harm.

Self-harm was bleak. It was a chaotic riot of feelings and emotions that couldn't be put into words or communicated effectively. Mental health professionals despaired at being told: "I don't know" every time they asked me why I did it or how it felt whereas I despaired at not belonging. I was too 'poorly' and too 'at risk' to be at home, but not 'mentally ill' enough to be in hospital. I slipped into - got stuck - in an empty chasm of nothingness; I couldn't recover sufficiently to live a reasonable quality of life outside mental health services so the only solution, in my twisted and distorted mind, was to become unwell enough to qualify for a starched white hospital bed.

The hospital removed all obvious 'sharps' from my belongings in order to 'keep me safe'. This I understand, but what I couldn't then grasp was how I was to manage without them, when they weren't replaced with anything? Hospital ward was busy, nurses spent most of each shift in the office doing paperwork and I was watched over by a varying selection of healthcare assistants, and many of those were often from an agency and didn't even know my name. If I was found to have an injury (for one doesn't need sharps or anything else in order to harm in times of desperation) I was told off. Reprimanded. When I eventually handed in a smashed plate I had been holding onto I was told off for damaging hospital property. Reprimanded again. It took a lot of courage to knock on the office door and hand it over, on the day I decided to try and stay 'safe'.

Discharge occurred when either they needed my bed or they simply didn't know what to do with me anymore. Fill me up with drugs and send me home.

Self-harmers hear the phrase 'attention seeker' a lot. Maybe I was, maybe I wasn't…does it matter? What was so hideous in my life at that time that the need to hack holes in my legs seemed like a good idea? Why was that the best way to cope? Being told we're 'doing it on purpose' or that we 'need to take responsibility for our behaviour' is also common. Yes, often harmers do injure consciously and yes recovery does involve having control over ones actions and finding less maladaptive methods of coping… we know that. What we don't know is *how*…how do you go about stopping?

Self-harm took on an addictive quality, to the point where the day didn't feel complete, or finished, without it. Addictive and habitual.

I don't remember the first time, and I can't recall the last…maybe it hasn't happened yet. How would one define recovery from self-harm? What is recovery? If mental health sits on a continuum of fluctuating symptoms, at what point on the scale is anyone deemed 'well'?

Am I better? Am I recovered?

That is open to interpretation.

INTERVENTIONS

This section will introduce some of the interventions both previously and currently provided by a range of services. Attitudes as an integral part of this process will also be incorporated into the overall intervention debate. As intervention may mean very different things to different people a specific meaning has been identified within this chapter for the purposes of clarity. Here intervention will be defined as:

'Anything that is employed by the individual and/or others to compromise the need to self-harm/injure, deal with the consequence of an episode of self-harm/injury biopsychosocially, or to support the individual irrespective of the intention or outcome.'

Literature that compares what people who self-harm/injure themselves regard as of value compared to what they are offered by a range of services will be identified. What the person who self-harms/injures might consider to be an intervention will be another aspect of this section that will be incorporated in the following pages.

Assessment:

A range of literature produced relating to Accident and Emergency departments in this country (Whotton, 2002; McElroy and Shepherd, 1999; Greenwood and Bradley, 1997) has emerged exploring a range of issues including proposed intervention strategies. These have included the offer of a psychosocial assessment (introduced within the NICE 2004 guidelines) to all people who present having self-harmed/injured.

Whyte and Blewett (2001) explored the comparison between assessment carried out by accident and emergency staff and that of a 'specialist deliberate self-harm (DSH) team' and concluded that the quality of the assessment by the DSH team was better but little was noted regarding whether this improved the overall experience of the person who had presented after self-harming/injuring.

Kapur et al (2008) in a large scale study noted that in the population of individuals who had presented after an incident of self-harm/injury, an offer of psychosocial assessment was more likely to be accepted if the individual was aged over 55, was currently involved in mental health treatment and had been admitted (medical ward) after an overdose. Those who were unemployed had utilised cutting as their method of self-harm/injury and attended outside normal hours were less likely to access assessment.

It is important to note that assessment, particularly if it is associated with the label mental health/psychiatric can be seen by the individual as threatening, particularly if not handled with a high degree of sensitivity on the part of the practitioner. This was indicated in one report (TheSite.org, 2009) as having triggered self-harm/injury through the process of being encouraged insensitively to talk about underlying issues to a practitioner who was also a stranger.

The previous point is reinforced in work by Kuehl (2008) who indicates that the foremost request reported by someone who had self-harmed/injured was to be listened to. This if facilitated can sensitively be incorporated into the process of assessment enabling the individual to explore, in their time and on their own terms, some if not all of the information being sought by the practitioner. In this way some if not all control is retained by the individual in the unfolding process.

Management of the individual:

Kapur et al (1998) indicated in their work that the management of people who had self-poisoned was lacking in consensus and that there was a low medical and psychiatric priority given to people who had taken an overdose. It concluded that more work needed to be undertaken to improve the historical and current (1998) arbitrary management of people who deliberately self-poisoned. Redley (2010) in an interesting qualitative piece indicates the use of avoidance on the part of some clinicians who assessed an individual after admission, to explore reasons behind that individual's self-harming/injuring, as a strategy to minimise any emotional involvement leading to a potentially negative impression on the part of the individual.

The University of Manchester's self-harm project (MASH) (2008) mentioned   previously has looked at the outcome for individuals who had presented at the accident and emergency department. They separated out management into that by emergency department (ED) staff and mental health specialists. The results indicated:

ED staff:
1. 21% were referred by ED staff to psychiatric services
2. 53% were admitted to a hospital bed
3. 15% received no referral
4. 3% self-discharged
5. 3% either told to or referred to their GP
[n=5887]

Mental health specialists:
1. 29% were referred to their GP
2. 14% urgently referred (mainly to crisis team)
3. 12% to other services (e.g. counselling, social services)
4. 7% resulted in admission to a mental health ward/unit
[n=2198]

[Adapted from 5.4 Management of episodes by Emergency Department and psychiatric staff, MASH project, 2008, p15]

The previous figures can be contrasted with figures produced in the National Registry of deliberate Self-Harm (2011) that indicated:

1. Admission (general) 30.1%
2. Admission (mental health) 10.7%
3. Left before any recommendation 14.7%
4. Were not admitted 43.7%

[n=11,966]

Admission:

The World Health Organisation (WHO) in the section on mental health has examined a variety of questions linked to self-harm including one related to the intervention of hospitalization of people who self-harm:

'Q6: Is hospitalization better than non-hospitalization for persons who self-harm?'

The recommendation was that this would not be recommended for non-specialised areas of a general hospital but would be appropriate for individuals requiring medical interventions as a result of the self-harm/injury and that they should be monitored closely whilst there to reduce the risk of further self-harm.

Sinclair and Green (2005) in their qualitative study identified that for some of their subjects that 'admission to hospital was remembered as a frightening experience which furthered their perception of a lack of control'. Even though numbers were quite limited the issue of control emerges as an important consideration. Perego (1999) in an earlier article indicates recognition that 'the optimum treatment for patients presenting with deliberate self-harm is no longer   enforced admission to a general hospital' (p26)

Alternatives to A&E:

An interesting observation is the mention of alternatives to the accident and emergency department for individuals who did not wish to attend hospital. A study conducted by Hume and Platt (2007) identified that some people felt uncomfortable repeatedly attending an accident and emergency department. This is echoed by Mackay and Barrowclough's (2005) who reported that the negativity staff reported towards individuals who presented repeatedly. An early piece of qualitative work by Harris (2000) explored the experiences of a group of women and noted in part that 'In this account, we can see an element of hostile care that was reported by several other women in this study. This is an attempt to embarrass the patient...' (p168).

Friedman et al (2006) again identified some negative and unhelpful attitudes among staff towards people who self-harmed/injured but rather surprisingly this also included more senior staff who had not received training in the area of self-harm/injury. Bryant and Beckett (2006) in their project were exploring the idea of an advocacy service for people who had self-harmed/injured and attended the emergency department. Although some people noted poor attitudes on the part of the staff, there was generally a positive response to the medical care received.

The development of community alternatives as a means of supporting individuals has emerged from a number of these studies as an alternative and one that increases the likelihood of some people seeking and continuing to access support when they self-harmed/injured.

A point that emerges from the statistics presented in the next section on management of the individual is one that indicates that up to one third of individuals (in the mental health figures) were referred to their GP. Houston et al (2003) identify the role as an important one in terms of familiarity with the family and associated social and health history. They also indicate that the GP is in a potentially unique position to offer a more holistic approach due to their relationship with the individual and family. One dissenting voice in this area is that of Bhardway (2001) who in her exploration of young Asian women and self-harm/injury identifies that in the young women who had been interviewed many expressed their concern regarding GPs and the maintenance of confidentiality. It was because of this concern that many indicated that they avoided their GP for fear that their families might be informed.

Another positive alternative view of this is posed in an article by Kerr et al (2010) who indicates that the family medicine/primary care physicians are in a unique position to intervene and can also be of value in the assessment and management process because of their relationship with the individual and family.

Psychosocial approaches:

An area that has increased in prominence in mental health care has been the utilisation of a range of 'therapies' usually under the umbrella term of psychosocial interventions. Guthrie et al (2001) looked at a brief psychodynamic interpersonal therapy that was facilitated in the individual's own home after their presentation at an accident and emergency department. There was a suggestion that there might be some value for the individuals involved. Crawford et al (2007) explored the use of psychosocial interventions following an episode of self-harm/injury but the context was one of prevention of subsequent suicide so has little relationship with this work.

Boyce et al (2003) in their article summarising the guidelines available from the Royal Australian and New Zealand College of Psychiatrists indicate that both Cognitive Behaviour Therapy (CBT) and Dialectical Behaviour Therapy (DBT) may have some value but linked to underlying mental health disorders. They also cautioned that in vulnerable individuals any 'in-depth' therapy may actually result in self-harm/injury following. Slee et al (2008) in a study identified that the use of short CBT (12 sessions) in additional to TAU (treatment as usual) demonstrated clear improvements although it is unclear what other elements were involved other than a mention of improvement in 'depression, anxiety and suicidal cognitions' (p208). The various limitations of the study are clearly identified by the authors.

Hazell et al (2009) in a study replicating earlier work explored the use of group therapy with adolescents who had self-harmed/injured. Their conclusions indicated a contradiction with earlier findings in as much as the benefit of group therapy over routine care was not demonstrated.

Feigenbaum (2010) indicates the possibility of DBT as an intervention that could assist in supporting individuals who have self-harmed/injured. Kerr et al (2010) suggest in their work that little evidence exists outside of the use of DBT in people with Borderline Personality Disorder (BPD) although they conclude with a statement that 'effective psychotherapeutic treatments are available for patients who self-injure' (p254). In the current draft version NICE (April 2011) in an analysis of the current evidence suggests that there might be some value in pursuing a short intervention (six sessions) structured explicitly for people who self-harm. They also suggest that although the current evidence suggests value that this needs to be explored through further research before any degree of certainty applies to the efficacy of utilising this form of intervention.

On a much broader base but worthy of mention is work by Chandler et al (2011) who suggest that if the fields of sociology, together with social and clinical sciences combined to research the topic then a less biased and more biopsychosocial understanding might emerge with resultant benefits for those individuals who self-harm/injure and those who support them.

Recovery model approach:

The recovery concept has its origins in the field of mental health and illness and developed in areas as diverse geographically as the United States and New Zealand. Although it has been considered as a significant addition to the 'thinking' in mental health it has not featured in self-harm/injury. The concept as outlined by the Scottish Recovery Network (SRN) states:

'Recovery is being able to live a meaningful and satisfying life, as defined by each person, in the presence or absence of symptoms. It is about having control over and input into your own life. Each individual's recovery, like his or her own experience of the mental health problems or illness, is a unique and deeply personal process.'

If we adapt this by altering very few words there are echoes that reflect similar aspirations within the context of self-harm/injury as indicated below:

'Recovery is being able to live a meaningful and satisfying life, as defined by each person, in the presence or absence of self-harm/injury. It is about having control over and input into your own life. Each individual's recovery, like his or her own experience of self-harm/injury, is a unique and deeply personal process.'

This then allows another perspective to emerge that is reflected in some of the other material explored that investigates the wishes, expectations and aspirations of people who have self-harmed/injured and come into contact with services, albeit primarily health. It is therefore conceivable that this model could be an appropriate one for consideration. It does not need to reside within the domain of an 'illness', physical or mental, but instead offers a clearer focus than already exists in some of the ideas mentioned in self-harm/injury literature to date.

Practitioners:

Pierce (1986), in one of the early articles published around the subject area identified a potential issue with lack of sympathy not only from professionals to whom an individual came for support and help but also from their family. He suggested this was an area that might be important to focus on in an effort to modify family responses and support the family member who was self-harming/injuring.

In 1998 Deiter and Pearlman indicated that self-harm/injury posed problems and challenges for practitioners in whom reactions such as 'anxiety, confusion, anger, helplessness, pity and desire to control the situation' (p236) were not uncommon. This had a tendency to alienate rather than engage the individual seeking advice, help and/or support.

Deiter et al (2000) in another article highlighted the importance of a collaborative engagement with the individual who has self-harmed/injured and a need to avoid any behaviour that adopts 'punitive or shaming responses'. The professional should instead seek consent from the individual, introduce themselves and 'be direct, honest and respectful of the patient' (p1182).

Hadfield et al (2009) identified in a small qualitative study that there still existed challenges in some of the attitudes of doctors (in this instance A&E) in engaging with people who self-harmed/injured. McHale and Felton (2010) again focused on staff attitudes and indicated that despite the range of literature published, together with recommendations and guidelines available, that there still exists: 'clear discrepancies between what service users and health care professionals view as positive or negative attitudes and how these affect care provision.' (p739)

Work by Huband and Tantam (2000) looked at attitudes amongst mental health staff and in a postal survey identified that one of the significant features that emerged was one of control. The staff who felt that the service user (in the work presented as a vignette) had more control were more negative in their responses. Wheatley and Austin-Payne (2009) explored staff attitudes from a mental health perspective regarding inpatients who self-harmed/injured and the staff who worked with them. Findings again suggested issues linked to such variables as experience and training that staff received. One additional outcome here was the recognition that unqualified staff were often involved in direct care and that they needed training and support, in an effort to improve their confidence and aid the development of a more positive experience for all concerned in the process.

Myer (2011) explores the issue of effective intervention and includes a range of ideas already mentioned by others but also suggests:

- do not force individuals into 'no self-harm' contracts
- encourage the identification of alternative coping strategies such as calling/texting family/friends
- offer relaxation techniques but as an option not requirement

The Royal College of Psychiatrists provide a range of readily accessible material related to self-harm/injury and their leaflet offers a range of available and possible interventions whilst admitting that evidence is still limited in terms of which are most effective. They include:

- talking with a non-professional
- self-help groups
- help with relationships
- talking with a professional
- family meetings
- group therapy

Service users:

The information presented previously in this chapter is interesting in as much as a minority of individuals were seen as requiring mental health specialist intervention, including admission. The needs of the service user in this context does not necessarily mean that the individual will be seen in an accident and emergency department or be admitted to hospital, but will access some help, advice and/or support from a 'service'. It is important to separate out the traditional view of a service user as someone primarily coming into contact with a health care organisation and instead consider service users as people who will access someone or something that they believe or expect to help them.

In a survey carried out by Outside the Box Development Group (2008) a substantial majority of those initially surveyed regarded self-harm/injury as part of a mental health and wellbeing issue rather than always part of a mental illness. Later in the report, a number of individuals indicated that they had not attended an accident and emergency department because they were concerned that they would either encounter a negative experience or might be detained in a psychiatric hospital (p15).

The Truth Hurts Report (2006) included a chapter (4) on support and therapeutic interventions and reflected what young people who participated thought might be of help. This included:

- support/counselling
- group support/drop-in
- self-help group (facilitated)
- creative initiatives
- multimedia/internet access
- information point

[Adapted from Table 3: What young people thought would be helpful, Truth Hurts, p58]

A rather unique account is offered by a qualified mental health nurse (anonymous, 2001) who also self-harmed/injured. The account indicated the most important 'interventions' related to the interaction between the people who self-harmed/injured and those who provided treatment and care. The following were cited as 'not cures' but of marked value:

- human touch
- some words of kindness
- being at ease in the presence of someone who had self-harmed/injured
- a genuinely caring and non-judgemental attitude

School-based:

Wishart (2004) in a report produced in a part of the Australian state of Victoria explored issues related to young people who self-harmed/injured and reported on schemes introduced to assist both teachers and the student in school environments. Two approaches mentioned included:

School 1 - the introduction of a protocol that included the following 'rules':
   a) students will be sent home if they self-harm at school
   b) students cannot attend class if they are bleeding
   c) students with recent scars must wear long sleeves to school
School 2 – the introduction of an "exit pass"
   a) students could exit class at any time when they felt upset, stressed or unable to cope with the classroom environment
   b) the student showed the card to their teacher and could leave the room
   c) they would then speak to a teacher previously nominated
It is worth noting the differences in approaches taken. Another point that was noted was that there appeared to be little abuse of the exit card by students and an acknowledgement that it appeared to help in the reduction of self-harming/injuring at the school.

Sullivan et al (2004) noted that in their survey of young people and mental health a significant theme that emerged was the amount of pressure that young people felt regarding schoolwork, together with parental conflict emerging as a commonly reported issue outside of school by young people who had self-harmed/injured

Adolescents:

The need for a specialist adolescent nurse has been discussed in recognition of the discrete attributes of adolescence. The need to assess the young person has been recognised prior to guidelines being issued but has not been a universal approach. Cook (1998) as an example identified a need to distinguish between unhappy and depressed through the use of an assessment tool. There is also an acknowledgement that the use of a 'psychiatric' tool or referral onto a psychiatrist may be counter productive due to the potential stigma. Schubotz (2010) in the Young Life and Times survey data identified that of those young people who self-harmed/injured 50% preferred a single professional to provide support and in the case of young people who were same-sex attracted this was a quite significant preference.

Martin et al (2010) advocate in their booklet that lists of alternatives to self-harm/injury as an intervention strategy may initially be discounted but in their discussions with young people identified that some things work for some people and that therefore they can serve a useful purpose. This can be either in the form of deferring the need to self-harm/injury to a later time or even resulting in the occasional outcome of not self-harming/injuring.

Older people:

One group that receives little attention is that of older people. Currently some of the media stories linked to stories about poor care provision for older people, primarily in either a hospital or care home environment is creating a degree of attention that is long overdue. In the context of self-harm/injury this is still an area that needs recognition to ensure that those individuals who are older and self-harm/injure are not overlooked in the current planning and provision. It is generally recognised that the number of older people who self-harm/injure is much smaller than in the younger age group but this does not mean that the need is any less. Mitchell and Dennis (2005) in their article identified that the majority (two thirds) of people who are known to self-harm/injure were under the age of 35. This however, indicates that there is another third who are over that age. In their epidemiological presentation the figures identified approximately:

- up to age 30   – approximately 2,000
- age 30 - 50   – approximately 2000
- age 50 +   -- approximately 400

This highlights that although there may be a greater number of people - who present having self-harmed/injured - who are younger that there is still an issue regarding older people and self-harm/injury.

Pierce (1987) identified that in a review carried out over some 12 years that of those older individuals who were in contact with a hospital having self-harmed/injured, some 90%+ had depressive conditions, 65% had a significant physical illness and 50% received psychiatric treatment. In a shorter-term study of 2 years Lamprecht et al (2005) indicated that in their identified population (82) that over 20% of the men had no discernible psychiatric diagnosis. Of potential significance was the fact that 58% of the individuals had visited their GP in the four weeks prior to the episode of self-harm/injury.

Dennis et al (2004) in their study compared a group of older people who had presented with depression and self-harm compared to a group with depression. They concluded that older people in this situation should be seen and assessed by mental health professionals with specific experience with older people.

Harm cessation v Harm minimisation:

A comparison between potential limitations and risks of harm-cessation versus the alternative approach of harm-minimisation is explored by Cadman & Hoy (2009). There emerged a gradual realisation that trying to prevent someone from self-harming introduced a potentially greater risk than working with someone and allowing self-harm/injury to take place if needed in a managed situation. The dichotomy between those who support harm-cessation or harm-minimisation continues to this day but there is now a greater awareness of the importance of supporting the individual and this requires including them in the process of what options may be available. Work published in this area over many years identifies the uncertainty and lack of evidence that continues in terms of 'what is best?'

A study by Morgan et al (1993) explored the potential benefits of using a green card (emergency card) for individuals who had presented having self-harmed/injured as a means of encouraging them to contact services should they need future help and support as a possible means of helping to reduce a repeat episode of the self-harm/injury. The outcome was regarded as significant after a follow-up after one year.

By way of contrast Kapur et al (2010) in an editorial determined that evidence was still insufficient. They explored the impact of various interventions used as a follow-up with someone who had self-harmed/injured. The use of postcards, green cards (sometimes known as crisis or emergency cards) and telephone calls have all been employed and although some success appears to have been achieved the evidence is still insufficient to draw clear conclusions. Further exploration of this approach is needed to determine if it could offer one element of support to the person who has self-harmed/injured.

The debate regarding the positive and/or negative elements related to the two approaches is best summed up as follows:
A). Associated with harm cessation are issues frequently perceived as counter-productive to the individual and their situation. As a counterbalance some of the potential reasons that may support the concept from the perspective of family and/or practitioners associated with the individual who self-harms/injures are

offered. These include those identified in figure eight below.

Figure 8: Harm-cessation

INDIVIDUAL	FAMILY/PRACTITIONER
disempowerment	empowers others who may feel helpless
stigma ('bad' behaviour = 'bad' person)	a need to assist stop/prevent an 'abnormal' activity
admission (or threat of) to a mental health unit	may persuade individual to consider stopping
refusal or discontinuation of treatment (if not stopped)	may persuade/force individual to stop
removal of any equipment associated with harm/injury	may help individual stop
use of a 'no self-harm/injury' contract (might be linked to treatment/access)	may persuade/force individual to reconsider and stop

B). By way of contrast harm-minimisation is often perceived as a more collaborative and less restrictive and threatening approach. It is intended to include the individual who self-harms/injures in the process of planning any interventions and may include elements identified in figure nine:

Figure 9: Harm-minimisation

INDIVIDUAL	FAMILY/PRACTITIONER
'supported' self-harming	empowers others who may still feel quite helpless
contact numbers/details for individuals/organisations	involvement in supportive process
access to information regarding self-help (e.g. first aid)	supportive role and possibility of reduced concern
education linked to medication (e.g. impact and effects)	awareness of need for specific information
retention of control, empowerment	partnership

It is important to stress that most practitioners who support the idea of harm-minimisation rather than harm-cessation do not see it as 'normalising' the activity but recognise that there may be the need to accommodate it to both support the individual in times of stress/distress and to reduce the stigmatisation associated with self-harm/injury.

Issues related to the individual and their involvement in the process of recovery are identified by Bell (2011) who indicates that the major contributory factors are;

- motivation
- openness and honesty with oneself
- an involved support system
- a commitment to treatment and self-care

In a systematic review of literature by Taylor and Hawton (2007) looking at attitudes and satisfaction, a similar pattern of information emerged to that mentioned previously; e.g. psychosocial assessment, staff sensitivity, education and training for clinical and non-clinical staff.

If we accept the premise that many people who self-harm/injure do not seek help or support from other people for a variety of reasons it may be of value to look at interventions and how they may evolve in terms of need and necessity. Figures one and two earlier in the book identify some of the varied reasons people may self-harm/injure as previously discussed. Together with this is the acknowledgement that subsequently, depending on the method used to self-harm/injure the individual may employ an intervention. This might consist of first aid, for example in the case of a burn or cut. If the method employed results in injury or harm that was not planned or anticipated then other interventions may be appropriate, including informing others and/or seeking help.

It is in the 'additional consequences' element that the situation may move from one that initially remained within the control and domain of the individual who self-harmed/injured towards a situation where external involvement becomes a matter of necessity rather than choice as suggested in figure four. This raises an interesting issue of the differing interpretations of intervention, what it is considered to be and who determines it. This introduces the need to be clear about the parameters related to a concept as characterised by my own interpretation introduced at the beginning of the chapter. If we open up the debate we then need to consider some of the many variables that will influence different views on the concept of intervention.

These may consider:

- Are we looking only at clinical/professional concepts of the term?
- Can anyone intervene?
- Is anything that may be implemented to assist the individual to avoid self-harm/injuring an intervention?
- Is something that is implemented after an episode of self-harm/injury an intervention?
- Is the help/support/advice provided by another to assist the individual to either avoid self-harm/injure or to minimise it considered intervention?

From the questions posed it becomes clear that the concept of intervention is not as simple as some people may initially consider it to be. The final question brings us on to the idea that intervention may be something that does not necessarily or always need the immediate physical presence of or access to others. This introduces the ideas of alternatives such as:

- Books (e.g. self-help; information sources)
- Internet (e.g. support groups; information sources; communication)

Accessing others (as mentioned above) as a support intervention strategy does not necessarily involve making direct (visual/physical) contact with someone known. This has been an important part of the Samaritans strategy for many years. Being able to communicate with someone without having to identify who you are and not having to relate in a face-to-face situation may be an important lifeline for some individuals. This has been developed by other groups in an effort to engage and support particularly young people.

In Australia headspace utilises 'eheadspace' which is identified as: 'a confidential, free, anonymous, secure space where you can chat or email with qualified youth mental health professionals if you are 12 to 25 years old.' This also may help to address the issue mentioned earlier regarding stigma and fear of mental illness and mental health professionals due to the anonymous and confidential nature of the service. The equivalent website in New Zealand [www.headspace.org.nz] has identified the challenge of identifying 'good' information on the web and has undertaken what they refer to as 'some surfing and come up with the following, which we think are cool for teenagers living in New Zealand to look at.' The site then provides a list of sites that provide a range of information, advice and support related to youth issues.

The role of the internet as an intervention is one that has historically been met with some scepticism and indeed hostility on the part of professionals. Early literature (and indeed some more recent material) has a rather ambivalent relationship with the internet as a possible positive concept. Morris (no date) in a   report available online explored the issues related to responsibility regarding websites and information indicating that when it comes to issues related to self-harm and eating disorders there are two types of web content and a clear distinction needs to exist between these, as follows:

1. websites that are designed to assist those who are trying to recover
2. websites aiding the continuation of destructive behaviour

Baker and Fortune (2008) identified the relationship that exists between some people who self-harm/injure and the internet. This was identified as something that practitioners needed to develop their understanding of because of the important relationships that some individuals who self-harmed/injured had with the internet as a source of information, advice and support. They also felt that practitioners needed to develop a more balanced and less negatively biased view in this area. Some information continues to offer both examples of what can be accessed through this medium. A lecture given at a conference (Green, 2007) has been placed on the internet and contains some interesting material together with a couple of quite graphic photographs of individuals who have cut themselves quite badly with no triggering warning noted on entry to the web page.

Prasad and Owens (2001) had some time previously explored the idea of the internet as a supportive mechanism and although they determined the evidence was not available they did concede that many groups, individuals and organisations did view this medium as a positive one. In the transcript of a presentation given by Dr Helen Keeley (no date) regarding teenagers and self-harm/injury she remarks about the support provided by a young woman who 'unfortunately has gone back to Australia to manage a very nice website called "Reach Out" which I recommend anybody who is interested in young people and their coping strategies to have a look at'.

It is interesting to note that although there is still some disquiet regarding the internet and whether it plays a positive or negative role as an intervention, a number of researchers are happy to use it as a medium to carry out research in this very area (e.g. Murray and Fox, 2006; Baker and Fortune, 2008).

It is also important to note that intervention, as previously mentioned, is a multi-facetted concept. It has traditionally been thought of in terms of someone who needs support, advice, treatment being facilitated by a professional (usually doctor or nurse) within a hospital based environment as noted by the references to accident and emergency departments in much of the associated literature. This has gradually been enhanced with the emergence of a range of alternative options as discussed within this chapter, including other professionals (e.g. teachers), voluntary groups or organisations (e.g. Samaritans), internet based groups (e.g. FirstSigns), and online forums and chatrooms. This, together with a vast increase in the amount of information that people can now access and utilise has to some extent helped to   reduce the isolation that some people have previously felt regarding their self-harming/injuring.

If we consider the model introduced in Chapter 2 (T.I.M.E.) then another consideration enters the debate and that is the individual themselves and the actions (or interventions) they consider and/or take when thinking about, undertaking or after a self-harming/injuring episode. The process identifies a three-step concept, namely:

1. BEFORE
2. DURING
3. AFTER

Although I have identified three components they are not meant to be considered as discreet entities but as part of a continuum, each one part of a much greater whole. In order to explore this in more detail it might be clearer to demonstrate this in the form of a diagram. This has been constructed and can be considered in the diagram (Figure 10) on the next page.

From the information presented in figure 10 we can determine that 'intervention' is something that the individual has a degree of control over throughout the three phases. This varies dependent on the need created by a situation that results in the individual considering self-harm/injury. At the initial point (before) the individual has a number of potential options but much will depend on their perception of what others might think or how they may react if involved through becoming involved. This could involve a range of different people including family, friends, colleagues, and/or professionals.

Confidential links are now more widely available as a means to circumvent this need for those who still want to talk to or engage with someone but not in a face-to-face contact and even considering the need to remain unknown to the person or group contacted (anonymous).

Figure 10: **Intervention as a self-related concept**

B **E** **F** **O** **R** **E**	A). Incident occurs that triggers thoughts of potentially self-harming/injuring B). Individual considers options that may be used to reduce the need to self-harm/injure including self-based, as well as possible use of others (including contact with other people) C). Strategy offers a range of potential options, not all of which would lead to self-harm/injury as an outcome (or that help to defer the decision)
D **U** **R** **I** **N** **G**	A). Self-harm is occurring B). Awareness of the degree of control that is retained by the individual important to reduce the risk of unwanted outcome (serious risk to self, potential unwanted involvement of others) C). The influence of previous point (B) determines the outcome, largely irrespective of the self-harm/injury method employed

A **F** **T** **E** **R**	A). Self-harm/injury has occurred B). Outcome has resulted in either a (i) resolution of the issue/event or has been compromised by an (ii) escalated risk due to the degree of harm/injury C). If outcome is (ii) then the involvement of others becomes a necessity rather than an option

The second phase (self-harming/injuring) will tend to reduce this consideration of others with a focus now centred on attempted resolution of the present situation or need. There is still an option for the individual based on their awareness of what is happening and to what extent they have control over the outcome. This might involve a more conscious and deliberate exercise based on ensuring that what is taking place is unlikely to result in a need to involve anyone else unless this is a voluntary decision. It might also incorporate the need to recognise when the situation is not controlled sufficiently to ensure a safe resolution and to have some means to alert others as a safety mechanism. This again could reflect some of the range of options discussed previously.

In the third phase the self-harm/injury phase has passed and some outcome has arisen. We may be in a situation where the individual may be distressed by what has happened but is less distressed than when the original trigger occurred. A less satisfactory outcome could be the realisation that the self-harming/injuring has resulted in harm or injury that has compromised the individual's welfare and requires attention to address the resultant health/physical issue. Again this still allows the individual to determine the intervention (in terms of who, when, where) but is less flexible because of the need for outside assistance.

The above issues demonstrate that intervention can be something that the individual him/herself can exercise a varying degree of control over and that this is important to recognise. It challenges the idea that intervention is the prerogative of others and instead introduces the idea that the individual can manage this process if provided with support from others in the recognition of this as an option. It offers a more distinct process than that explored in figure eleven on the following page that is based on a more traditional perception of intervention

Figure 11: Self-harm/injury – outcome and intervention

Physical (external): [can be potentially seen, detected by others]	Physical (internal): [cannot be easily seen or detected by others]
<ul><li>cutting</li><li>burning</li><li>scalding</li><li>hair pulling</li><li>biting</li><li>scratching</li><li>picking wounds using a ligature</li></ul>	<ul><li>overdose of medication</li><li>insertion of object(s) into orifices or under skin</li><li>swallowing objects</li><li>swallowing toxic substances</li><li>fractures</li></ul>
Psychological outcome: (consequence)<ul><li>Relief</li><li>Release</li><li>Emotional 'calming'</li><li>Guilt reduction</li></ul>	Psychological outcome: (consequence)<ul><li>Relief</li><li>Release</li><li>Emotional 'calming'</li></ul>

• I exist	• Guilt reduction • I exist
Physical outcome: (consequence) • tissue damage • blood loss • tendon/ligament damage • hair loss • infection	Physical outcome: (consequence) • tissue damage • organ damage • blood loss • infection
Additional Consequences: • First aid (personal) • Telling others (due to need for assistance) • First aid (other) • Accident & emergency attendance • Hospital admission • Mental health referral	Additional Consequences: • First aid (personal) • Telling others (due to need for assistance) • First aid (other) • Accident & emergency attendance • Hospital admission • Mental health referral

In terms of the value of the internet as an intervention and whether this is ultimately a good or bad consideration is summed up quite nicely in an interesting statement that exists on the PsychCentral website placed by an individual who is designated as a 'Chat Leader'. In this part of the site there is a 'self-injury room' where individuals who self-harm/injure can communicate. The ambivalence of feeling towards the Internet as a vehicle that can either be positive or negative is summed up in the welcome statement:

'I'm often a little wary or concerned when asked to create this forum, because I'm afraid that it will feed the self-injury behaviour rather than be a support or help to its members'

Despite the reservations stated above it is acknowledged frequently that support websites can be an important resource for young people who are generally very comfortable with technology (unlike some of their older family members and indeed professionals they might encounter). TheSite.org (2009) published research based on an evaluation of the development of its site as a source of advice and support. There was an indication that young people made use of websites for support and advice based on a number of factors that included the convenience of readily available access, confidentiality and anonymity. Provided there was effective moderation of the use of such websites it was seen as an important part of the resource option for young people.

One element that is overlooked by some of the literature is the impact of self-harm/injury on family, friends and colleagues of the individual. The need for this important group of people to be supported, advised and informed is identified by Bywaters and Rolfe (2002) and this in turn is seen as important in the support that they can then potentially offer the person who is self-harming/injuring. Byrne et al (2008) also identify the important role of the family as an antecedent in children and adolescents' self-harm/injury but also the need to support both the young person and family as an important part of the recovery process. The need to educate parents to enable them to support the individual who self-harmed/injured was identified by Schubotz (2010) as in the data produced, young people indicated that 40% of the young people who self-harmed/injure indicated their mother was aware of it.

Summary:

It is evident from the material that intervention is a complex concept. It may within a traditional professional context be considered as something that they (the professionals) facilitate. This now can take many different approaches from hospital based (e.g. A&E; admission to general and/or mental health care) to community based provision, including GPs. Alternatives to this have been explored including web-based alternatives such as forums and chatrooms and availability of information and advice that can be accessed both immediately and if desired anonymously. There is also the idea that the individual who self-harms/injures has a significant role in determining who, what, where and when (or not) will be involved.

References:

'Anonymous' (2001) Self-harm keeps me alive, *Openmind* 111, Sept/Oct, p10

Baker D, Fortune S (2008) Understanding Self-Harm and Suicide Websites: A Qualitative Interview Study of Young Adults Website Users, *Crisis: The Journal of Crisis Intervention and Suicide Prevention*, Volume 29, Number 3, pp118-122

Bell H (2011) Self-injurious behavior: Learning new ways to cope, *The Morning Sun*, Michigan

Bhardwaj A (2001) Growing Up Young, Asian and Female in Britain, *Feminist Review*, Number 68, pp52-67

Boyce P, Carter G, Penrose-Wall J, Wilhelm K, Goldney R (2003) Summary Australian and new Zealand clinical practice guideline for the management of adult deliberate self-harm (2003), *Australasian Psychiatry*, Volume 11, Issue 2, pp150-155

Bryant L, Beckett J (2006) *The Practicality and Acceptability of an Advocacy Service in the Emergency Department for People Attending Following Self-Harm*, University of Leeds

Byrne S, Morgan S, Fitzpatrick C, Boylan C, Crowley S, Gahan H, Howley J, Staunton D, Guerin S (2008) Deliberate Self-harm in Children and Adolescents: A Qualitative Study Exploring the Needs of Parents and Carers, *Clinical Child psychology and Psychiatry*, Volume 13, Number 4, pp493-504

Bywaters P & Rolfe A (2002) *Looking beyond the scars: Understanding and responding to self-injury and self-harm*, London, NCH

Cadman L & Hoy J (2009) *Cutting the Risk: Self-Harm Minimisation in Perspective – Teaching and learning Guidelines*, Mind, p29

Chandler A, Myers F, Platt S (2011) The Construction of Self-Injury in the Clinical Literature: A Sociological Exploration, *Suicide and Life-Threatening Behavior*, Volume 41, issue 1, pp98-109

Cook A (1998) Assessing deliberate self-harm: A team approach, *Emergency Nurse*, Volume 6, Number1, pp21-24

Crawford MJ, Thomas O, Khan N, Kulinskaya E (2007) Psychosocial interventions following self-harm, *The British Journal of Psychiatry*, 190, pp11-17

Deiter PJ and Pearlman LA (1998) Responding to self-injurious behavior. in Kleespies PM (Ed) *Emergencies in Mental Health Practice: Evaluation and Management*, New York, The Guildford Press

Deiter PJ, Nicholls SS, Pearlman LA (2000) Self-Injury and Self-Capacities: Assisting an Individual in Crisis, *Journal of Clinical Psychology*, Volume 58, Number 9, pp1173-1191

Dennis M, Wakefield P, Molloy C, Andrews H, Friedman T (2004) Self-harm in older people with depression:

Comparison of social factors, life events and symptoms, *British Journal of Psychiatry*, 186, pp538-539

Dickson S, Steeg S, Gordon M, Donaldson I, Matthews V, Kapur N, Cooper J (2011) *The Manchester Self-Harm Project: Self-Harm in Manchester January 2008 – December 2009*, University of Manchester

Feigenbaum J (2010) Self-harm – The solution not the problem: The Dialectical Behaviour Therapy Model, *Psychoanalytical Psychotherapy*, Volume 24, Issue 2, pp115-134

Friedman T, Newton C, Coggan C, Hooley S, Patel R, Pickard M, Mitchell AJ (2006) Predictors of A&E staff attitudes to self-harm patients who use self-laceration: Influence of previous training and experience, *Journal of Psychosomatic Research*, Volume 60, Issue 3, pp273-277

Green B (2007) Deliberate Self-Harm: The Breadth and Scope, available at http://priory.com/psych/DSH.htm

Greenwood S, Bradley P (1997) Managing deliberate self-harm: The A & E perspective, *Accident and Emergency Nursing*, 5, pp134-136

Guthrie E, Kapur N, Mackway-Jones K, Chew-Graham C, Moorey J, Mendel E, Marino-Francis F, Sanderson S, Turpin C, Boddy G, Tomenson B (2001) Randomised controlled trial of brief psychological intervention after deliberate self poisoning, *British Medical Journal*, Volume 323, pp1-5

Hadfield J, Brown D, Pembroke L, Hayward M (2009) Analysis of Accident and Emergency Doctors' Responses to Treating people Who Self-Harm, *Qualitative Health Research*, Volume 19, Number 6, pp755-765

Harris (2000) Cutting the bad out of me, *Qualitative Health Research*

Hazell PL, Martin G, McGill K, Kay T, Wood A, Trainor G, Harrington R (2009) Group Therapy for Repeated Deliberate Self-Harm in Adolescents: Failure of Replication of a Randomized Trial, *Journal of the*

American Academy of Child & Adolescent Psychiatry, Volume 48, Issue 6, pp662-670

Houston K, Haw C, Townsend E, Hawton K (2003) General practitioner contacts with patients before and after deliberate self-harm, *British Journal of General Practice*, May, pp365-370

Huband N, Tantam D (2000) Attitudes to self-injury within a group of mental health staff, *British Journal of Medical Psychology*, 73, pp495-504

Hume M, Platt S (2007) Appropriate interventions for the prevention and management of self-harm: a qualitative exploration of service-users' views, *BMC Public Health*, 7:9,

Kapur N, Cooper J, Bennewith O, Gunnell D, Hawton K (2010) Postcards, green cards and telephone calls: therapeutic contact with individuals following self-harm, *The British Journal of Psychiatry*, 197, pp5-7

Kapur N, House A, Creed F, Feldman E, Friedman T, Guthrie E (1998) Management of deliberate self poisoning in adults in four teaching hospitals: descriptive study, *British Medical Journal*, 316, pp831-832

Kapur N, Murphy E, Cooper J, Bergen H, Hawton K, Simkin S, Casey D, Horrocks J, Lilley R, Noble R, Owens D (2008) Psychosocial assessment following self-harm: Results from the Multi-Centre Monitoring of Self-Harm Project, *Journal of Affective Disorders*, Volume 106, Issue 3, pp285-293

Keeley H (no date) Deliberate Self-Harm in Teenagers, Presentation, available at http://www.3ts.ie/downloads/transcripts/helen%20keeley.pdf

Kerr PL, Muehlenkamp JJ, Turner JM (2010) *Nonsuicidal Self-Injury: A Review of Current Research for Family Medicine and Primary Care Physicians*, Journal of the American Board of Family Medicine Volume 23, Number 2, pp240-259,

King M, Semlyen J, See Tai S, Killaspy H, Osborn D, Popelyuk D, Nazareth I (2008) A systematic review of mental disorder, suicide, and deliberate self-harm in lesbian, gay and bisexual people, *BMC Psychiatry*, Volume 8:70, www.biomedcentral.com/1471-244X/8/70

Kuehl S (2008) Emergency Department Re-Presentations Following Intentional Self-Harm, MSc Thesis, Victoria University of Wellington, available at http://researcharchive.vuw.ac.nz/bitstream/handle/10063/641/thesis.pdf?sequence=2

Lamprecht HC, Pakrasi S, Gash A, Swann AG (2005) Deliberate self-harm in older people revisited, *International Journal of Geriatric Psychiatry*, Volume 20, Issue 11, pp1090-1096

Martin G, Hasking P, Swannell S, McAllister M, Kay T (2010) *Seeking solutions to self-injury: A guide for young people*, Centre for Suicide Prevention Studies, The University of Queensland, Brisbane

Mackay N, Barrowclough C (2005) Accident and emergency staff's perceptions of deliberate self-harm: attributions, emotions and willingness to help, *British Journal of Clinical Psychology*, 44, pp255-267

McElroy A, Sheppard G (1999) The assessment and management of self-harming patients in an Accident and Emergency department: an action research project, *Journal of Clinical Nursing*, 8, pp66-72

McHale J, Felton A (2010) Self-harm: what's the problem? A literature review of the factors affecting attitudes towards self-harm, *Journal of Psychiatric and mental Health Nursing*, 17, pp732-740

Mental Health Foundation (2006) *Truth Hurts: Report of the National Inquiry into Self-harm among Young People*

Mitchell AJ, Dennis M (2005) Self-harm and attempted suicide in adults: 10 practical questions and answers for emergency department staff, *Emergency Medicine Journal*, 23, pp251-255

Morgan HG, Jones EM, Owen JH (1993) Secondary prevention of non-fatal deliberate self-harm. The green card study, *The British Journal of Psychiatry,* 163, pp111-112

Morris E (no date) *Self-Harm in the Digital Age*, Family Online Safety Institute

Murray CD, Fox J (2006) Do internet self-harm discussion groups alleviate or exacerbate self-harming behaviour? *Advances in Mental Health*, Volume 5, Issue 3, pp225-233

Myer T (2011) Inside Intentional Self-injury, *Nursing*, 26-31

National Suicide Research Foundation (2011) *National Registry of Deliberate Self Harm Annual Report 2010*, Cork, National Suicide Research Foundation

NICE (2011) *Self-harm: longer-term management in adults, children and young people*, Draft for Consultation (April 2011)

Outside the Box development Support (2008) *Adults' experiences of self-harm*, Glasgow

Perego M (1999) Why A & E Nurses Feel Inadequate I managing patients who deliberately self harm, *Emergency Nurse*, Volume 6, Number 9, pp24-27

Pierce D (1986) Deliberate Self-harm: How Do Patients View Their Treatment? *British Journal of Psychiatry,* 149, pp624-626

Pierce D (1987) Deliberate Self-Harm in the elderly, *International Journal of Geriatric Psychiatry*, Volume 2, Issue 2, pp105-110

Prasad V, Owens D (2001) Using the internet as a source of help for young people who self-harm, *Psychiatric Bulletin*, 25, pp222-225

Redley M (2010) The clinical assessment of patients admitted to hospital following an episode of self-harm: a qualitative study, *Sociology of Health & Illness*, Volume 32, Issue 3, pp470-485

Schubotz D (2010) *The mental and emotional health of 16-year olds in Northern Ireland: Evidence from the Young Life and Times survey,* Patient and Client Council

SRN (2009) Recovery: What is Recovery, Scottish Recovery Network, http://www.scottishrecovery.net/What-is-Recovery/what-is-recovery.html

Sinclair J, Green J (2005) Understanding resolution of deliberate self-harm: Qualitative interview study of patients' experiences, BMJ, doi:10.1136/bmj38441.503333.8F

Slee N, Garnefski N, van der Leeden R, Arensman E, Spinhoven P (2008) Cognitive-behavioural intervention for self-harm: randomised controlled trial, *The British Journal of Psychiatry*, 192, pp202-211

Sullivan C, Arensman E, Keeley HS, Corcoran P, Perry IJ (2004) *Young People's Mental Health: A report of the findings from the Lifestyle and Coping Survey*, Cork, The National Suicide Research Foundation

Taylor TL, Hawton K (2007) *Attitudes towards and satisfaction with services among deliberate self-harm patients: A systematic review of the literature*, NCCSDO

TheSite.org (2009) *Self-Harm: Recovery, Advice and Support – Exploratory and evaluative research*

WHO (no date) Mental Health: Hospitalization for persons who self-harm, www.who.int/mental_health/mhgap/evidence/suicide/q6/en

Whotton E (2002) What to do when an adolescent self harms, *Emergency Nurse*, Volume 10, Number 5, pp12-16

Wheatley M, Austin-Payne H (2009) Nursing Staff Knowledge and Attitudes Towards Deliberate Self-Harm in Adults and Adolescents in an Inpatient Setting, *Behavioural and Cognitive Psychotherapy*, 37, pp293-309

Whyte S, Blewett A (2001) Deliberate Self Harm: The impact of a specialist DSH team on assessment quality, *The Psychiatrist,* 25, pp98-101

Wishart M (2004) *Adolescent Self-Harm: An Exploration of the Nature and Prevalence in Banyule/Nillumbik*, Nillumbik Community Health Service, p38

Additional Contributors

The following section contains some more examples of the most important element of the book. It once again steps outside the previous exploration of literature, research and terminology and instead has as its focus the real experience of self-harm/injury.

The stories that have already been provided within the book together with the following are representative of the experiences of individuals who over the past year have come forward and volunteered their unique version of what self-harm/injury means for each of them and how it has entered and influenced their lives. It is important to again emphasise that the stories provided by each individual remain true to the original contribution.

The range and diversity of people who have offered their stories and the content of the actual stories themselves help to clarify that self-harm/injury is not confined to a particular gender, age or ethnicity, nor can it necessarily be easily explained in terms of what may have created the original 'need' to self-harm/injure.

I remain eternally appreciative of the courage of each individual in their placement of trust in a person they did (indeed do) not know, namely me! A number of stories arrived through third party contacts that had been informed and involved in the process of asking for volunteers. Others made contact directly via email having heard/encountered information regarding the planned undertaking.

The contacts would not have been possible without the assistance of a number of online groups/organisations who were extremely supportive and provided information in a variety of formats to enable individuals to become aware of the original request.

J [age 30]

I was twenty-three when I first started self-harming, although I had experienced periods of poor self-care before then such as not allowing myself food, or taking risky routes home from work. There were several reasons for my choosing to express my distress in this way, but the main trigger was due to being date raped when I was a teenager while studying away from home. I had grown up with an abusive alcoholic father also, which meant that I feared my own anger, showing it in ways that might frighten others.

At the core of it all was my inability to express negative emotions and my anger at my body for letting me down when I needed it to protect me from my attacker. I had disassociated myself from my body, and no-longer saw harm that was done to it, as really being harm to myself. I most commonly chose to self-harm by cutting my forearm using razors when they were planned incidents and anything sharp that was around, when I was overwhelmed and in the spur of the moment. I did also overdose on painkillers every so often, however, not in a bid to end my own life, just as another way to damage my body that I was in control of. Self-harming actually helped me to stay alive during a very distressing and difficult time in my life. It meant that I was able to express the anger, frustration and emotional pain that I had in a controlled and secretive manner.

I had tried talking to others about my sexual assault, but the people I told were unable to cope because they didn't know what to say or do to help me. I didn't always have the words to explain what was going on in my mind. At points, I actually looked forward to self-harming, the adrenaline rush that came with the pain, allowed me to feel something other than my ongoing depression and anxiety. I took pleasure in shopping for plasters and taking care of wounds immediately after cutting. It seems ironic now, but I took pleasure in also having the opportunity to show myself care. Once the incident was over and my emotions were more settled, I would feel relieved and able to breathe more easily, however, within a few hours I would be disgusted at myself for not having the strength to stop harming and would always promise that I would not do it again. Harming kept my mind occupied. If I wasn't taking part in the act itself, I would console myself with the thought that if I failed one of my classes or if I made a mistake, I could hurt myself later. I was always looking for new ways to hide my injuries, make up new excuses for wearing long sleeves in the summer etc.

After some time, I acknowledged that I wanted to stop feeling the need to harm myself and I started to look for help. This was terrifying   because self-harm is not something which people easily understand and often I would see their reactions to my scars as their disgust of me as a person. Initially, I looked for help and information online as I could remain anonymous. I decided to write a journal entry every time I felt like harming myself. At first I would write about giving in and how good it felt, but over time, just writing about my feelings would either make the extent of the cutting less, or prevent it from happening altogether. This, however, did not help me in situations where I was forced to make instant decisions and did not have the opportunity to write about how I was feeling.

My friends were aware of my emotional difficulties and I later found out that they knew I was self-harming, but they felt powerless to help me. At the time, I felt as though they didn't care and even if they had confronted me, I would have lied. My relationships with my family members were almost non-existant as I had stopped talking to them some time before. I felt that no-one could relate to me, therefore, I shut myself off from them. There was no way that I felt that I could admit to my self-harm to those I worked and trained with, as teachers hold positions of care and authority of others, and I couldn't even take care of myself. The secretive nature of it all, made it easier to lead a double life, but harder to admit that I needed help.

Over the decade that I experienced mental health difficulties, I have come across medical professionals that have caused my healing both help and harm. The majority of healthcare workers, who were older, treated me with what I perceived as disdain and clearly thought that my self-harm was 'attention seeking and immature' as it seems to be widely accepted that self-harm is the hobby of bored teenagers. Unfortunately, those experiences, just gave me more ammunition when harming myself afterwards. I can say, however, that the positive, supportive and honest reactions of one male Community Psychiatric Nurse changed my life. He treated me like an equal human being, respected me in spite of my shortcomings and made me feel as though he cared about my welfare. In times where I hated myself and wanted to harm, I would manage to resist because I did not want to let him down.

I spent six months working with him on learning Cognitive Behavioural Therapy techniques which meant that my negative thoughts regarding myself were slowly overcome. Over the months and years that followed, I kept up the momentum and went from being a shy, almost invisible person, to being proactive and confident. The self-harming did not disappear totally, but realizing that someone else believed that I could overcome it, and that it was just a poor choice of coping mechanism, nothing more, gave me the drive I needed to keep moving forwards. I eventually found the strength to face up to my rape through two years of psychotherapy, something I would never have been able to do before. This enabled me to go on to have healthy sexual and emotional relationships, heal the rifts with my family and gave me the confidence to help pupils who were struggling emotionally themselves. The hurdles I overcame have actually made me a more emotionally resilient person and through my work, I seek opportunities to teach children how to maintain good mental health in a bid to remove some of the stigma.

Although I have not self-harmed in several years and I consider myself 'cured' the urge will appear every now and then. I realise that I needed to self-harm to stay alive, and it served its purpose. Self-harming is just an alternative to other 'coping mechanisms' such as turning to drugs or alcohol, taking anger out on others etc. It is not shameful, nor weak. Now that my scars have faded to silvery lines, although they remain very noticeable, I have some affection for them. They are the physical evidence that I endured an emotional battle and survived. They no longer embarrass me and I do not feel the need to hide them, even when I am teaching in school. Although I was aware of alternatives to cutting such as snapping an elastic band on the wrist etc, I did not find any of them helpful in my recovery. My addiction to harming was powerful and the only way I was able to overcome it was to want something that was bigger than my need to self-harm. In the end, it was my dogged determination and my want to meet my potential that led to my recovery, once I had been given the tools to managing my emotions. I will be forever grateful to the CPN who literally helped me to change my life.

Lo [age 21]

Over the years I have been through so much. I do not want to focus on what I have been through though, because even though it may be important...what really counts is the path to recovery...a path that I am still walking along!

A brief overview though. Growing up with my parents wasn't always the greatest. At times my parents, especially my Dad was abusive towards me and my siblings. Sometimes it was physical, but more often it was verbal. Many times I got very scared about being home, and that's when the nightmares and panic attacks started. Towards the end of 2004 I was sexually abused by my Grandpa. I still do not remember how things got to that stage and how I managed to keep seeing him for months on end, until my parents finally found out...but then I guess that the coping strategies I had adapted, such as self-harm helped a lot with that. Six months after being sexually abused, I was molested by my first boyfriend. I was a mess. How could everything bad keep happening to me? When would it all just finally end?

Over the years I have struggled greatly with both an eating disorder and self-harm. I have also been diagnosed with severe depression and borderline personality disorder. I don't mind being labelled, although the BPD label got to me a lot. I still remember when I was first diagnosed with it. It felt like it was a lifelong sentence; it was something that could never fully be taken away from me...all I could do was learn to deal with it to the best of my ability.

As I have already mentioned, self-harm was one of the coping strategies that I used greatly over the years. For me it just worked so well. It enabled me to feel in control - free. By cutting, I felt so alive. I never liked how other people could just hurt me and get away with it. Or the fact that they could do it whenever they pleased, without anyone knowing. By cutting, I realised that I could control when I was hurt, how much pain I was in. It was my way to not focus on what was really going on, that being that I had been mistreated badly and had been hurt in the most horrific ways.

When people hear about self-harm, many assumptions are put forward straightaway. Things like, only attention seekers do it, that by self harming the person is trying to take their own life, and so many other things. This is not true though.

What people don't realise, is how quickly self-harm can become an addiction. I remember when I first started on that sunny afternoon 6 years ago. I kept telling myself that it was ok, that if I didn't want to do it anymore then I could just stop, just like that...but I was dead wrong.

What started as only cutting once a week, turned into cutting every day, and from cutting every day turned into cutting any spare minute I had, including at school and on my breaks at work. On many occasions I was almost found out by my parents and friends. But no matter how much I wanted to stop, I just couldn't. I needed to self-harm in order to feel alive; I needed it to stay alive.

Over time though, I realised how much self-harm had taken over my life. I was withdrawing from everyone, I could no longer have fun, I couldn't even be touched or hugged by others...in fear that they would find me out.

In countries all over the world, there are always some kind of helpline that can help start the recovery process with you. With me living in Australia, I used Kids Helpline, a private and confidential phone service for young people – I still use them greatly today.

Making that first call was one of the hardest things I have ever been faced with. Because by calling, I was admitting I needed help, and by saying that, I was also breaking through my own walls to possibly let another person in to help me.

I was very, very lucky with the first counsellor I touched based with, she was amazing and I actually remember one day extremely well. I had a very strong urge to self-harm and something in me convinced me to try talking with her first. I had my tools and everything out that I needed, but the important part of this story is what I did throughout the phone session...instead of hurting myself, I destroyed my tools!! I didn't realise I was doing it, but when I clicked, the feeling was bliss!

Since that day, 5 years ago I have been able to let numerous health professionals into my life. Some experiences with telling them about my self-harm was absolutely horrible, but as someone quite close once said to me "if the first person you tell doesn't listen or know how to help you, try someone else... somewhere along the line you will always find that perfect person!"

I am female. I am only 21 years old. I started to self-harm when I was 15yrs old. I wish I had never made that first cut. But I strongly believe that no matter what we may face as human beings, we are always able to take back the control and make our lives better. I strive best at my recovery when I am helping others or doing things that may help those people I may not even know. This is why I help out at First Signs. And in the future I hope to make an even bigger difference!

M [age 19]

Hi. I'm M. I'm a 19 year old female student from South Wales. I was sexually assaulted by my best friend in February of last year. A month later, things became too much to deal with on my own and this was the first time I turned to self-injury. I'm not sure why I did this at first. I just know that my thoughts were overwhelming. I felt trapped within my emotions, like I was losing control of everything and there was no escape. Everything around me was slipping away from me. My colleague was talking about sexual abuse and unbeknown to him was seriously triggering me. I'd spend hours at a time in my room alone, without a clue what was going on. I was scared and would just rock back and forth. Whenever this would happen, if someone spoke to me, I wouldn't hear a thing they were saying. The first time I took the blade, I felt such an amazing relief. Like I could finally let a small amount of that pain out.

There were many reasons I carried on doing this. Sometimes I felt nothing at all, I felt completely empty. So this was a way of being able to feel something, anything. Other times I'd be angry. Angry at myself for not getting out of the situation in the first place, for allowing such a thing to happen to me. I'd be angry for not being a stronger person. Whilst some may say I was being the opposite of strong by giving into the urges to self-injure, it was never about regaining that kind of strength. It was almost as if I was punishing myself even further. That by punishing myself I could forgive myself for getting into that place. I was also so angry at him and as I couldn't take my anger out on him and taking it out on anyone else would be unfair, I had no option but to take it out on myself. I felt by injuring myself, it calmed me down without interfering in anyone else's life.

But most importantly, self-injury is and always has been a form of control for me. When your head is all over the place, when you lose control in such a big way, sometimes any control is better than none. Even if that means hurting myself to gain back that control. I lost so much that night, it hurts a lot knowing that someone who was supposed to be my best friend wouldn't listen to me saying no, took every ounce of control from me and I would do anything to get that back. I was going through so much emotional distress, questioning everything that has ever happened in the duration of our close relationship, questioning everything I did and if there was anything I could've done differently that night. Calmness washed over me every time I self-injured, my racing heart beat slowing down to a normal pace again. My feelings were back in control again, even if just for a few moments. The pain I was feeling was because of something *I* had done, not because of a decision someone else had made.

However, it soon became addictive. As it had such an instant, intense calming effect, I found myself doing it more and more. A lot of the time I would get anxious throughout the day if I hadn't had the opportunity to be alone and self-injure. It was becoming my addictive habit, something I did on a daily basis, sometimes more than once daily, the calmness was like a drug to me.

I've had mixed responses from people who have found out about the self-injury. Most of the time it was unintentional that they found out. I sometimes wish it could have been in better circumstances but then I guess there aren't really any good ways to find out someone you know self-injures. My male best friend, who is now my partner, found out through an online message board. He was finding it difficult to understand my depressive feelings so I sent him on a board I had recently written on, forgetting I had also posted about the self-injury. As soon as I realised what I had done, I begged him not to read the rest of my posts. But it was too late. Luckily he was supportive. He was hurt and upset I could do such a thing. But, whilst he struggled to understand exactly why, he did and still does do his best to support me.

A few months later, I told one of my female best friends about it who, aside from the self-injury, has been there through some of my worst moments. Her response totally shocked me. She was completely understanding and showed me her scars from a few years previously. I was upset that she'd felt that low but glad she has found the strength to overcome it. She told me that I will stop when I feel ready, no sooner, no matter what anyone else tries to tell me. One of the best comments about it I've ever received was from one of my close male friends when I was upset about the scars. He said; "I know you self-harm M, it's no wonder. But you'll always be beautiful to me." That actually made me cry because it was such a lovely thing for him to say and really means a lot he thinks that.

Things have also gone the other way. My mental health nurse demanded to see and told me I was stupid and should stop. That really hurt! Two reasons, one, because she was so blunt about it, no one had ever seen my cuts before; it was always my little secret. And two, because a trained professional, - someone who is supposed to understand - called me stupid. I know full well it's not the ideal coping method, but if it was that easy to stop, I would've have done it already. To be honest, she just made me feel worse about myself and want to do it even more; "I'm a stupid girl that needs to be punished!" That's how she made me feel about it.

My new counsellor is so much better. Of course, she asks if I have self-injured recently or if I have thought about it but she never makes a big deal out of it. Instead, she chooses to focus on resolving the issues behind it all.

I don't actually know exactly what made me stop so much. For some reason I just realised I couldn't carry on like this. I tried all sorts of things to distract myself. But when I did slip up, I'd beat myself up about it and feel so bad. I've come to realise now that it doesn't matter if I slip up. It's great if I can distract myself, but it's not the end of the world if I can't. My main trigger now is anxiety. The anxiety inside builds up and up until I can't take it anymore. Often, I'll try going for a run to take my mind off things or listen to happy music. But sometimes things just become too much. I realise I still have a long way to go but I've found talking out about my issues can help a lot. It's a common misconception that self-injury is about attention seeking. It has never, ever been about that for me. I used to hate, even fear, the thought of someone knowing about this. But if talking to a close friend helps, telling them about my need to self-injure and the feelings behind that, I can't see how that is a bad thing.

DISCUSSION

The previous chapters of the book have attempted to explore some of the many and diverse issues related to the topic of self-harm/injury, through an exploration of some of the multitude of information that exists and the inestimable contribution of those individuals who provided their unique experiences. It might now be the time to try and identify some of the elements that have emerged and what we might have determined from this.

1. What is self-harm/injury?

An exploration of the literature, internet, conversations with colleagues and individuals who have self-harmed/injured and the stories provided in this book result in an awareness that the answer still eludes me. Interpretations from all of these sources are many and diverse. The concept would appear to range from something that is considered within an anthropological construct as 'normal', albeit not practiced by all; an unhealthy but necessary coping strategy that is used by some people to deal with issues in their lives, to a deviant behaviour that requires some degree of external intervention to discontinue.

What is apparent is that the current state of our knowledge and understanding is such that we are still some way from determining a clear understanding that will result in acceptance by all the interested and involved parties. The variation that currently exists from the information available demonstrates the degree of difference that can be identified and the challenge that awaits any effort to construct a single explanation that everyone will be happy to subscribe to.

That does not mean we should not continue to ask the questions or indeed upset some of the vested interests in this pursuit. What is important is that we do not lose sight of the central purpose of this; i.e. the individual who self-harms/injures needs understanding, acceptance, recognition and support while they consider the options available to them, including self-harm/injury.

2. Why do people do it?

Once again another question that initially invited the search for an answer through an exploration of the available information. Unfortunately the answer was complicated as the information explored contained a significant range of possible and some probable explanations for why people might self-harm/injure. Ultimately there appears to be a degree of consensus that people might engage in self-harm/injury as a result of some significant event in their life that created a need for resolution that was not possible through any other means.

It is important to note that other people might not appreciate the degree of significance that the event might have for the individual. What may be deemed insignificant by one person may be considered very significant by someone else. This is something that needs to be acknowledged in our attempt to understand and learn from the experience of others.

Less positive perceptions of the agenda that people who may be self-harming/injuring are addressing through their actions such as attention seeking and manipulative interpretations appear to be less frequently alluded to now than in earlier literature. It is important that just because some individuals perceive these to be negative that all the alternatives are also acknowledged. This, if considered, can lead to a more positive interpretation of these expressions and therefore the person associated with them. 'Attention seeking' might be more appropriately considered as 'attention needing' and manipulation is one method of either communicating a need or exercising some control in a situation when little by way of alternatives are available to the individual. This is reflected to some extent in a piece written by Bhardwaj (2001) who indicates that rather than being perceived as attention-seeking self-harm/injury may act as a catalyst for change.

3. Self-harm/injury and suicide

This section explored the relationship that is frequently identified within much of the professional literature. It is acknowledged that a number of individuals who self-harm/injure are at greater risk of attempting or completing suicide later in their life. What is less clearly identified is an analysis of the other many variables that may be present including mental illness. There is also an acknowledgement that many individuals do not access or utilise services such as accident and emergency departments and/or mental health services so there is an unknown population that has not necessarily been vectored into the statistics of risk that are frequently cited within some of the literature explored.

It is important to recognise that some people might be more vulnerable and that there might at some point in their life be an escalated risk but this should not cloud peoples' judgement and suggest that anyone who self-harms/injures is likely to attempt or complete suicide. This would have the potential of further alienating and distancing individuals form the very services that might otherwise have a positive role in their survival and recovery.

It is also noted that some of the available information provided both through the literature and stories provided has acknowledged that the activity of self-harm/injury has had a very clear agenda that was focused on using this strategy as a vehicle to continue with life and manage the many situations that may arise, including challenging ones.

4. Interventions

Within this section we were looking for evidence that helped to determine those strategies that helped individuals who self-harmed/injured. What arose instead was an interesting identification of some of the ambiguity associated with the meaning of 'an intervention'. The initial focus was centred on interventions related to the person who self-harmed/injured but it soon became obvious within some of the material that this was not always the interpretation being considered. What emerged as a potential alternative was the question of who the intervention was for.

In terms of helping were we talking about the individual who self-harmed/injured or were we talking about others (e.g. professionals, family, friends, colleagues)? This only became clear in looking at literature that explored issues such as attitudes of professionals, for example, and identified that the experience encountered by the individual who self-harmed/injured depended on a range of other variables. These were seen to be determined by such issues as education, training, understanding and the professionalism of the practitioner. These elements are both extrinsic (provided by the organisation) and intrinsic (self-awareness and empathy) so are reliant on both the place and the person.

A diversity of different approaches exist which range from treatment (related to mental illness for example) to psychosocial interventions (e.g. cognitive behaviour therapy) that can be provided both face to face and online where the individual can determine the pace of their completion of the programme. The utilisation of forums, chat rooms and self-help groups also have a role in this process and enable a choice for the individual who self-harms/injures. It must be emphasised however that to utilise and potentially benefit from any of these interventions the individual needs to communicate with someone else, directly or indirectly to enable the opportunity for intervention to occur.

Some of the literature identified that lack of engagement and use of available resources by the person who has self-harmed/injured has occurred through poor experiences, the fear of being considered mentally ill and then referred to that service, potentially doubling the stigma (i.e. self-harmer/injurer + mentally ill). It is refreshing to note that community based services are now becoming an option in some areas in an attempt to reduce this concern based on its primary association with accident and emergency departments.

It might be appropriate to finish this element with the fact that much more time and effort is now being invested in helping people at a much younger age (preferably in upper primary or early secondary school) to consider the invaluable role of communication. Much of the access to or exclusion from help and support is determined by communication. Anything that helps individuals to develop a greater awareness and ability to communicate more readily can only be considered in a positive light. Much of the focus linked to this is based on the principal that men, in particular, struggle to communicate when they need help.

The message that is simple to state but not always utilised in time of need considers two crucial strategies:

1. If in need of help – ask someone
2. If you see someone else in need of help – tell someone

5. Stories

The previous section reflects a diversity of individuals, experiences and responses by these individuals to their specific circumstances. The stories are unique to the individuals who volunteered them and therefore not transferable to anyone else. It is for other individuals to determine the similarities and differences that these stories have in the context of their lives and experiences. It is, however, possible to identify some of the various issues that may create the environment in which self-harming/injuring becomes something that the individual may utilise to   address their distress.

There are no generalisations that can be taken from the stories that have been volunteered in terms of research applicability. We can consider that for each person involved, something took place at some point(s) in their life that resulted in self-harm/injury becoming a part of that person's life. There are however some elements that can be reflected upon both from an individual perspective and related to the literature that preceded the stories section.

These include:

1. Self-harm/injury is not confined to young people exclusively. The individuals who told their stories have an age range of 14 to 58 years

2. Self-harm/injury is not a 'fad' that people explore, dabble in and then move on. Although this has been suggested in an information sheet by Whitlock (2010) in terms of school settings it is balanced with the recognition that for many people self-harm/injury is a very private act. We need to acknowledge that for a very small minority of individuals this might be an issue but for many people that self-harm/injure this is something that may continue for some time. The

average length of time that the individuals represented in these stories have been involved with self-harm/injury was twelve years.

3. Self-harm/injury is not confined to females only. Women may be more inclined to discuss issues with someone else than their male counterparts and this tends to hide the true numbers of males who self-harm/injure. This is again reflected in the stories section and a range of published literature.

4. Intervention is one area that has a degree of correlation between the stories and previous information presented. There is recognition that any negative reaction or approach by other people, including professionals can have a marked impact on the individual and their motivation to seek support, help and advice. Some of the individuals, however, have also identified the importance and value of an individual who was non-judgemental and prepared to listen to them. Each individual's journey is quite unique and this point again needs to be remembered.

5. Although some individuals have considered a number of alternatives, including suicide, this is not something that has emerged as a consistent theme within the stories. This is in contrast to much of the professional literature that appears to have difficulty in separating self-harm/injury from suicide, at least in terms of what has been written and the inclination to draw comparisons rather than explore differences more explicitly.

6. Mental illness and links to self-harm/injury are apparent from both the literature and the stories

provided. It is again important to clarify that although some individuals indicated that they had had a mental illness and received help, support and treatment, others did not and their self-harm/injury was related to circumstances within their social and personal life. It is also important to consider that mental illness and self-harm/injury may be part of an individual's life but not necessarily at the same time and also not necessarily linked.

7. The role of family and friends can impact in both a positive and negative fashion. This is reflected within both the stories and literature. Some stories actually incorporate both elements due to experiences and this helps to indicate that although 'bad' things might happen and result in behaviour such as self-harm/injury that 'good' things can also happen and therefore hope is an essential ingredient in the process.

There is little indication that self-harm/injury is an issue that will reduce or change within the foreseeable future. There are signs that a reduction in the number of people presenting for help/support/treatment has taken place over the last couple of years but whether this is indicative of a reduction in the number of people self-harming/injuring or of an increase in the number of people not coming forward remains unclear.

It is apparent that professionals who have an important role in supporting, helping and treating individuals who self-harm/injure are responding to the criticism that existed regarding awareness, attitude and interventions. The inclusion of the topic not only in material traditionally aimed at informing and educating people (e.g. books, journals) but extended to the internet and a number of popular programmes on television has helped to increase this awareness, if not acceptance.

This also has helped to some extent to reach other people whose role in the life of the person who self-harms/injures is more important; i.e. family. As has been seen from some of the material presented, the role of the professional although important is likely to be transient. Other people within the individual's life will have a much greater impact over a much longer period of that person's life. Helping these individuals to develop a greater insight, awareness and acceptance is an essential part of helping the individual who self-harms/injures.

Education is recognised as one of the most important mechanisms in reducing issues such as discrimination, exclusion and intolerance. Continued exploration of the many issues associated with the topic of self-harm/injury will help to maintain this area in the public domain. Ignorance creates the opportunity for misinformation to become a prominent part of peoples belief systems and this is no different for the area of self-harm/injury. As mentioned previously there are a number of myths that appear frequently and associated with this area. It is fortunate that many of these are now used by support groups and organisations as examples of inaccurate and inappropriate information to educate people about the facts, not the myths (e.g. self-harm is attention seeking behaviour)

One of the issues that emerged from this work is an awareness of the need that people have to label anything that requires attention. It is something that although we may have difficulty in accepting is used as an integral part of our need to identify! The difficulty in this context is that it introduces a number of rather confusing issues such as those of:

- What label shall we use and who decides on it?

- What does the label convey or imply?
- Is everyone with that label considered to be the same or similar?
- Is the label for purposes of inclusion or exclusion?
- Is the label social, individual, clinical, political?

From these we can determine that labels have a range of potential uses and that these are not always positive. Perception and interpretation may be different for different people and this can lead to some of the issues that this book has attempted to include. It is essential that although we may require labels to identify for example groups and/or cultures, that ultimately we are dealing with individuals and that this must be the primary focus when attempting to support an individual who self-harms/injures.

It is important that we remember that we are dealing with a unique being and that although we may be following guidelines, protocols, advice, or interventions aimed at groups (in this context people who self-harm/injure) that some or much of the material we have at our disposal may not relate or apply to that person. It then becomes our responsibility to listen to and seek advice from that person to enable us to support and help more effectively.

Change is something that societally is generally evolutionary rather than revolutionary so it is important to consider that attitudes take time to adapt to new information and awareness. Progress has been made and should continue to be made. This in turn should encourage more individuals to explore a range of opportunities that will continue to emerge and provide both them and those involved with them a more positive experience and outcome.

References:

Bhardwaj A (2001) Growing Up Young, Asian and Female in Britain, *Feminist Review*, Number 68, pp52-67

Whitlock J (2010) What is self-injury? [Fact Sheet] Cornell Research program on Self-Injurious Behaviour in Adolescents and Young Adults
http://crspib.com/factsheet_aboutsi.asp

Resources

The following list has been compiled to reflect the large range of information and advice/support that can be found in the modern world of technology via the internet. It is not intended to be a definitive list of all the services, organisations, groups, or agencies that exist or the most appropriate but an illustration of the profile that self-harm/injury now commands in the wider community. The following list is presented alphabetically for convenience and not priority:

www.betterhealth.vic.gov.au
[Better Health Channel – Victoria; Australia]
www.bpdworld.org
[Borderline Personality Disorder site – information on self-harm]
www.casip.org.uk
[Cardiff Adult Self Injury Project]
www.crpsib.com
[Cornell University – Cornell Research Programme on Self-Injurious Behaviour in Adolescents and Young Adults – range of information]
www.firstsigns.org.uk
[FirstSigns]
www.fortysecondstreet.org.uk
[42nd Street – focus on young people under stress, includes self-harm]
www.harmless.org.uk
[Harmless –user led organisation with support, information and training linked to   topic of self-harm]
www.headspace.org.uk
[National Youth Mental Health Foundation – Australia]
www.healthyplace.com/Communities/Self-Injury
[HealthyPlace – America's Mental Health Channel]
www.helpguide.org
[HELPGUIDE.org – information, support and advice provided, including self-harm related]

www.insync-group.ca
[INSYNC – Interdisciplinary National Self-Injury in Youth Network Canada]
www.lifelink.org.uk
[lifelink – Glasgow centred with information and support related to self-harm]
www.mind.org.uk
[Understanding self-harm booklet available online]
www.nice.org.uk
[National Institute for Health and Clinical Excellence – guidance documentation linked to self-harm and its assessment and management]
www.nshn.co.uk
[National Self harm Network]
www.nhs.uk/conditions/Self-injury/Pages/Introduction.aspx
[NHS choices – Self-harm]
www.penumbra.org.uk
[Penumbra – Scottish mental health charity: includes self-harm information]
http://ie.reachout.com/inform-yourself/suicide-and-self-harm/deliberate-self-harm/
[ReachOut.com – information on self-harm]
www.recoveryourlife.com
[Self-harm support community]
www.rcpsych.ac.uk
[The Royal College of Psychiatrists – information on self-harm is available on the site]
www.samaritans.org
[Information related to self-harm available]
www.freewebs.com/sashpen
[S.A.S.H. (Survivors of Abuse and Self-Harm) – website set up by Linda as a resource for people who self-harm/injure]
www.seemescotland.org.uk
[seeme – Scotland, Self-Harm]
www.self-injury.com

[S.A.F.E. {Self Abuse Finally Ends} – explores issues related to self-injury and cessation]
www.selfinjurysupport.org.uk
[Self-injury support – Bristol Crisis Centre for Women]
www.siriusproject.org
[Information site compiled and maintained by a previous self-harmer]
http://www.spunout.ie/health/Healthy-mind/Self-harm
[SpunOut – Irish website aimed at young people]
www.supportline.org.uk
[Supportline – confidential support by telephone, email, post]
www.thecalmzone.net
[Campaign Against Living Miserably – aimed primarily at supporting young men]
www.thesite.org/healthandwellbeing/mentalhealth/selfharm
[TheSite.org – Self-Harm: Recovery, Advice and Support]
www.thewishcentre.org.uk
[Self-help peer group for girls aged 13-19, southern England]
www.users.zetnet.co.uk/bcsw
[Bristol Crisis Women's Centre]
www.youngminds.org.uk
[YOUNGMINDS – range of information, training available related to self-harm]

The following section contains a range of material that can be accessed online and reflects the wealth of material. It has as its focus a range of substantial and/or informative material produced in accessible format from a variety of different countries. The material is available via the indicated links and is presented with those most recently published introduced first and related to specific country:

United Kingdom:
http://www.rcpsych.ac.uk/files/pdfversion/CR158.pdf
[Royal College of Psychiatrists (2010) Self-harm, suicide and risk: helping people who self-harm – Final report of a working group]
http://www.patientclientcouncil.hscni.net/publications/index/reports
[Patient and Client Council, Publications: Reports. 20.10.10 mental and emotional health of-year olds in Northern Ireland]
http://www.cawt.com/Site/11/Documents/Projects/Self_Harm/Self-Harm_Registry_2009_Annual_Report.pdf
[Public Health Agency (2009) Northern Ireland Registry of Deliberate Self-Harm – Annual Report 2009]
http://www.healthscotland.com/documents/27.aspx
NHS Health Scotland (2009) *talking about self-harm*, booklet
http://www.selfinjurysupport.org.uk/files/docs/hidden-pain/hidden-pain-full-report.pdf
[Heslop P, Macauley F (2009) hidden pain? Self-injury and people with learning   disabilities, Norah Fry research centre]
http://www.youthnet.org/wp-content/uploads/2011/03/self-harm-exploratory-and-evaluative-research.pdf
[Self-Harm: Recovery, Advice and Support – Exploratory and evaluative research, June 2009]
http://www.injuryobservatory.net/documents/suicide_wales_2008_2013.pdf
[Welsh Assembly Government (2008) Talk to me: A National Action Plan to Reduce Suicide and Self-Harm in Wales 2008-2013]
http://www.otbds.org/assets/uploaded_files/project/SH_summary_report.pdf
[Outside the Box (2008) Adults' experiences of self-harm: Summary report]
http://www.mind.org.uk/help/diagnoses_and_conditions/about_self-harm_a_guide_for_young_people

[MIND (2008) About self-harm: Why you self-harm and how to seek help]
http://www.rcpsych.ac.uk/PDF/Self-Harm%20Quality%20Standards.pdf
[Royal College of Psychiatrists (2006) Better Services for People who Self-Harm: Quality Standards for Healthcare Professionals]
http://www.mentalhealth.org.uk/publications/truth-hurts-report1/
[Mental Health Foundation (2006) Truth Hurts Report]
www.dhsspsni.gov.uk/phnisuicidepreventionstrategy_action_plan-3.pdf
[Department of Health, Social Services and Public Safety (2006) Protect Life: A Shared Vision]
http://www.mentalhealth.org.uk/publications/the-truth-about-self-harm/
[Mental Health Foundation (2006) The Truth About Self Harm booklet]
http://www.statistics.gov.uk/downloads/theme_health/Childselfabuse_v1.pdf
[Meltzer H, Harrington R, Goodman R, Jenkins R (2001) Children and adolescents who try to harm, hurt or kill themselves, HMSO]

Ireland:
http://www.nsrf.ie/reports/CurrentStudies/YoungPeoplesMentalHealthReport.pdf
[Young People's Mental Health – A report of the results from the Lifestyle and Coping Survey]
http://www.nsrf.ie/reports/2010AnnualReportNationalRegistryOfDeliberateSelfHarmIreland.pdf
[National Registry of Deliberate Self Harm Ireland – Annual Report 2010]
http://www.nsrf.ie/reports/Bulletin/ResearchBulletin052011.pdf
[National Suicide Research Foundation – Research Bulletin May 2011]

Australia:
http://www.suicidepreventionstudies.org/uploads/ANES
SI%20Report%20Publication.pdf
[The Australian National Epidemiological Study of Self-Injury (ANESSI), 2010]
http://www.suicidepreventionstudies.org/uploads/A%20
Guide%20for%20Young%20People.pdf
[University of Queensland (2010) Seeking solutions to self-injury: A guide for young people]
http://www.livingisforeveryone.com.au/IgnitionSuite/uplo
ads/docs/LIFE-Fact%20sheet%208.pdf
[LIFE (2007) Deliberate self-harm and suicide, Fact Sheet 8]
http://www.health.gov.au/internet/main/publishing.nsf/co
ntent/C98FF0AF4A6CFF82CA2572610013A236/$File/s
elfharm.pdf
[The Royal Australian and New Zealand College of Psychiatrists (2005) Self-harm]

New Zealand:
http://www.tepou.co.nz/file/Research-
projects/suicide/evaluation-of-the-nzgg-self-harm-and-
suicide-prevention-collaborative-report.pdf
[Ministry of Health (2010) Prevention Collaborative: Whahawhanaungatanga (Phase 2 Evaluation – Final Report]
http://www.moh.govt.nz/moh.nsf/pagesmh/10482/$File/s
uicide-facts-2008-dec2010.pdf
[Ministry of Health (2010) Suicide facts: Deaths and intentional self-harm hospitalisations 2008, Wellington, Ministry of Health]

United States:
http://aacap.org/page.ww?name=Self-
Injury+in+Adolescents&section=Facts+for+Families
[American Academy of Child & Adolescent Psychiatry (1999) Self-Injury in Adolescents No73]

http://www.actforyouth.net/publications/results.cfm?t=sel
f-injury&d=1
[ACT for Youth Center of Excellence (2011) – Self-injury
material x2]
http://www.selfinjury.com/resources/journals/
[S.A.F.E. Alternatives – Journal Articles & Books – a few
accessible]
http://www.dsm5.org/ProposedRevisions/Pages/propos
edrevision.aspx?rid=443
[American Psychiatric Association – DSM-5
Development. V01 Non-Suicidal Self Injury]

Self-Harm/Injury

www.ingramcontent.com/pod-product-compliance
Lightning Source LLC
Chambersburg PA
CBHW031159270326
41931CB00006B/334